HOW TO HAVE A

BIG

WEDDING

ON A

SMALL
BUDGET

3RD EDITION

CUT YOUR WEDDING COSTS
BY HALF—OR MORE!

DIANE WARNER

BETTERWAY BOOKS

CINCINNATI, OH

Acknowledgments

I want to thank all of you throughout the country who gave so generously of your time and expertise to help me update this book for its third edition, and a special thanks to those professionals who helped me assemble the helpful tips for the groom, as well.

Special thanks to all those brides and grooms who shared their ideas with me during my seminars and through their interesting letters.

Finally, thanks go to my editor, Donna Collingwood, and my production editor, Marilyn Daiker, for their conscientious efforts to get this expanded book to the printer on schedule. It was a monumental task, I know, and I thank you both.

How to Have a Big Wedding on a Small Budget. Copyright © 1997 by Diane Warner. Printed and bound in the United States of America. All rights reserved. No part of this book may be reproduced in any form or by any electronic or mechanical means including information storage and retrieval systems without permission in writing from the publisher, except by a reviewer, who may quote brief passages in a review. Published by Betterway Books, an imprint of F&W Publications, Inc., 1507 Dana Avenue, Cincinnati, Ohio 45207. (800) 289-0963. Third edition.

Other fine Betterway Books are available from your local bookstore or direct from the publisher.

01   00   99   98   97   5   4   3   2   1

Library of Congress Cataloging-in-Publication Data

Warner, Diane.
  How to have a big wedding on a small budget / by Diane Warner.
    p.   cm.
  Includes index.
  ISBN 1-55870-448-5 (alk. paper)
  1. Weddings—United States—Planning. 2. Consumer education—United States.
3. Shopping—United States.   I. Title.
HQ745.W37 1997
395.2'2—dc21   96-40041
                               CIP

Edited by Donna Collingwood
Production edited by Marilyn Daiker
Cover designed by Sandy Conopeotis Kent
Cover photography by Pamela Monfort/Bronze Photography
Interior illustrations by Suzanne Whitaker

Betterway Books are available for sales promotions, premiums and fund-raising use. Special editions or book excerpts can also be created to specification. For details contact: Special Sales Manager, F&W Publications, 1507 Dana Avenue, Cincinnati, Ohio 45207.

To Ron and Lynn
Thank you for letting
me tell your story.
I love you.
Mom

Table of Contents

Introduction: There's Gonna Be a Wedding!

(Getting Over the Initial Shock)

So, there's going to be a wedding! Isn't that wonderful news? No? Maybe not? Of course, everyone is happy that the lovely woman has found the man of her dreams. Are you that woman? Or the mother of the bride? If the upcoming wedding makes you nervous, the problem is probably money!

If your family finances resemble those of the average American household, you never quite managed to save the money for a wedding. Or, perhaps you are already in debt, and now you discover that you'll need $18,000—the average cost of a wedding in the United States today, which is a slight drop from the $19,000 average quoted in the last edition of this book; this decrease is due to our recent recession and brides spending smarter and doing some of the work themselves.

At age twenty-five, our daughter found Mr. Right. He was a fine man, thirty years old, who was also waiting for the right one to come along. They had known each other for two years, both having been active in the Singles' Club at our local church. They had worked on committees together, gone on retreats together and seen each other at least twice a week, but always in large groups. Then, on the last day of May, he asked her out on a real date. At 6 P.M. they went to dinner at a little Italian restaurant, and by 10:30 P.M. they were still there, taking turns talking as fast as they could. They realized that they had everything in common—even astronomy—and before long they were spending evenings in our backyard, studying the stars with our daughter's telescope.

They saw each other every day and it wasn't too much of a surprise when they announced their engagement that August. They wanted to get married at Christmastime! How "storybook" precious! Right? Wrong! I had the same sense of dread you are feeling right now, only I didn't have the benefit of a book like this one to help us plan within our limited budget.

We were living on my husband's income from teaching at a

private school, and although I was working, too, my paychecks were being used to help our son through law school. We had decided that when our son graduated we would save all my paychecks toward any eventual weddings. Our daughter hadn't met the right guy yet; surely, we still had time to save. Of course, the timing didn't work out quite that way, but Lynn and Ron had a beautiful wedding anyway—and the price never came close to the national average. In chapter twelve there is a detailed breakdown of the expenses for our daughter's wedding that will show you how we cut costs, and by following the money-saving ideas in this book, you will be able to plan a wonderful wedding—even if you have a very small budget.

When we first knew that we would need to plan and pay for a big wedding with only four months' notice, my reaction, after the initial shock, was to go to the city library to search for information. I checked out eleven books, hoping they could give us a grasp of what this wedding would cost. I also asked various people for names of other families who had recently given weddings for their daughters. The library books were very thorough in explaining what is proper and what is not. They told about the hundreds of things to be done and when they should be completed. They told about traditions and trousseaus, gift registries and receiving lines.

Meanwhile, friends related hair-raising stories of a wedding photographer who arrived late, a best man who never arrived at all, a bridal veil that caught fire from a lighted candle, and a groom who fainted as the bride walked down the aisle. All these stories seemed quite amusing to the storytellers, but didn't seem a bit funny to me at the time. In fact, none of the information helped soothe the initial anxiety over the *real* question—how much will it cost?

We had so little time and I felt frustrated. Other inquiries were discouraging at first, too. One of the photographers I called, for example, had prices *starting* at $2,500!

It was through these first fumblings that I discovered that there was not a single book on the market that gave actual costs of a wedding in today's real dollars and cents, much less one that explained ways to stay within a tight budget. That was when I began taking notes for this book, which will spare you, I hope, all the frustrations I felt in those first few weeks of uncertainty. In chapter twelve you will find several sample budgets within various price ranges, along with four examples of recent weddings in which the brides managed to spend less than $3,800.

This book was not written for the family who can write a check a day between now and the wedding, hire a personal wedding consultant and pay for all the services the consultant recommends. I am happy for families who can do this; it makes things much easier. The bride (or Mom) doesn't have to act as her own wedding consultant, and she doesn't have to study a book like this one, which was written for families who must squeeze an entire wedding out of the "Food & Miscellaneous" budget. But I'll tell you a secret: If you use the ideas in this book, people will assume you did write a check a day, for there are many money-saving tricks that can be used to create an elaborate-looking wedding.

This book was not written for the family who will be satisfied with an intimate little wedding in the living room with twenty guests and a cookie and punch reception. Or to perpetuate the time-worn joke about holding the cost of the wedding to the price of a ladder—just give it to the groom and let them elope!

This book *is* written for the bride who wants a large traditional or contemporary wedding. She wants to feel very special for this one day in her life, with the walk down the long aisle of a beautifully decorated church or synagogue filled with her family and friends. Or, perhaps she dreams of a fragrant garden wedding or an elegant ceremony on a cliff overlooking the ocean. You *can* plan a wedding like this, no matter how tight your budget, but you will have to be, among other things, your own wedding coordinator. That means you will need to have all the facts and you will need to be very, very organized. This book will give you these facts and help you get organized and stay that way right up to the satisfying moment when you kick off your shoes and smile in relief, knowing it is all over and that it went well.

About This Book

When I began researching for this book, I collected every newspaper and magazine article I could find that gave me statistics or information that would help. I talked with everyone who knew anything about weddings, including recent brides. The most enlightening and voluminous information, however, came from the hundreds of interviews I conducted with retailers and wholesalers all over the country.

First of all, I sent out requests asking for prices, policies, pictures, catalogs and suggestions; I also conducted telephone and personal interviews. The information gathered into piles that filled the tops of two desks and five card tables, as well as a good part of the floor in my large writing room. Every new fact whetted my appetite for more. My small "music" pile, for example, soon ballooned with responses from musicians' unions, church and synagogue staffs, disc jockeys, entertainment companies, talent agents, amateur performers, university music departments, rental establishments, music stores, electricians, organists and sound engineers.

My home has a mail slot in the front door; the mailman shoves all the mail through the slot and it cascades onto my entryway floor. The returned responses came sailing through the slot at such a resounding rate that I could hear them from anyplace in the house. If I happened to be in the laundry room, I knew the mail had arrived when I felt the foundation shake. (Well, it wasn't quite that bad.) But there was definitely more information out there than I ever suspected. It was not only exhilarating and exciting, but a bit frightening when I contemplated condensing it all into one book. I had stuff from florists, caterers, wedding consultants, bridal salons, rental stores, bakeries, photographers, floral supply houses, wholesale food outlets, photo labs, tuxedo rental shops, delicatessens, cake decorators, seamstresses and fabric shop managers. I had notes on scraps of paper, the backs of catalogs and the margins of price sheets.

I spent many days in personal one-on-one research. I would leave the house in the morning, briefcase and notebook in hand. My husband would ask, "Where are you off to today?"

I would reply, "To Sacramento—florists and photographers." I interviewed the staffs at floral supply houses who gave me lessons in corsage making; photographers explained the virtues of Ektar 125 film. Fabric shop managers helped me assemble wedding veils and I actually tried on wedding and bridesmaids' dresses at rental shops, checking for quality and fit. When I came home each evening, I could hardly carry all the loot; I had catalogs, brochures, samples, pictures and boxes full of product information. I bravely unloaded it all into my "research room," carefully placing each item on its proper pile.

I divided the continental United States into nine areas, and came up with the average costs for everything from flowers to wedding gowns, from reception food to photography. These cost comparisons are included throughout the book, so you can get an accurate idea of how much things run in your area.

Find your state on this list:

KEY:		NE	=	Northeastern	CM	=	Central Mountain
SE	= Southeastern	NW	=	Northwestern	CA	=	California
SW	= Southwestern	MW	=	Midwestern			

Alabama	SE	Louisiana	SE	North Dakota	CM
Arizona	SW	Maine	NE	Ohio	MW
Arkansas	SE	Maryland	NE	Oklahoma	MW
California (Except	CA	Massachusetts	NE	Oregon	NW
Los Angeles and		Michigan	MW	Pennsylvania	NE
San Francisco)		Minnesota	MW	Rhode Island	NE
Colorado	CM	Mississippi	SE	South Carolina	SE
Connecticut	NE	Missouri	MW	South Dakota	CM
Delaware	NE	Montana	CM	Tennessee	SE
Florida	SE	Nebraska	CM	Texas	SW
Georgia	SE	Nevada	SW	Utah	CM
Idaho	NW	New Hampshire	NE	Vermont	NE
Iowa	MW	New Jersey	NE	Virginia	SE
Illinois	MW	New Mexico	SW	Washington	NW
Indiana	MW	New York (Except	NE	West Virginia	NE
Kansas	MW	New York City)		Wisconsin	MW
Kentucky	MW	North Carolina	SE	Wyoming	CM

CALIFORNIA METROPOLITAN: Greater Los Angeles Area; San Francisco Bay Area
NORTHEASTERN METROPOLITAN: Greater New York City Area; Washington, D.C.

As I did my research, I noticed that the prices in California and the Northeast were not uniform—the metropolitan areas have much higher costs than the other cities. That is why I added a "metropolitan" category for each of these regions.

Canadian Prices

In researching Canadian prices, I found them to be highest in the western and central-eastern cities. The Prairie and Atlantic Provinces were the lowest. If you live in the west, use my Northwestern States' costs as guidelines. The central-eastern cities can use the Northeastern States' costs. If you live in the Prairie or Atlantic Provinces, the Midwestern States' costs come closest to your own.

In every case, you need to adjust the prices by the exchange rate, which will add 18 to 20 percent to the U.S. cost guidelines.

If you live close to the border, it may be worthwhile to shop for certain items in the United States. Residents of Vancouver, for example, like to shop in Bellingham, Washington. There you can find turkey for about $1.30 less per pound than in Canada. I spoke with a resident of Florenceville, New Brunswick, who drives seven miles to the nearest American town to purchase her turkey and other dairy and poultry items. I mention turkey in particular because it is a main ingredient of one of my economical reception buffets (explained in chapter six).

Other items you may find at a lower cost in the United States are wedding gowns, shoes and tuxedo rentals. I found the identical tuxedo, for example, renting for $150 in New Brunswick as compared to $85 over the border.

All in all, Canadian weddings and receptions are traditionally longer and more elaborate than those in the U.S., which means that you need my cost-cutting ideas more than anyone.

In any case, use the average costs for your area as points of reference; after all, how can you cut down on expenses if you don't know what they normally run?

New Wedding Trends

Since the last edition of this book, there have been several new and dramatic changes in wedding trends which we will discuss throughout this book, including:

- ❧ A move away from Cinderella *fluff* to sophisticated elegance.

- ❧ Seventy percent of all couples are now paying for their entire wedding themselves.

- ❧ Destination weddings.

- ❧ More candid photo shots.

- ❧ Donating leftover reception food to food kitchens for the poor.

- ❧ Food stations at receptions (instead of long buffet tables), and Capuccino and Espresso bars in place of alcoholic beverages.

- ❧ Interesting alternatives to the standard limousine.

- ❧ Fewer pastels and more deep, bold colors, such as hunter green, burgundy, navy blue and black.

- ❦ Couples writing their own vows.

- ❦ The older the bride, the more informal the wedding (only 14 percent of brides over the age of 36 have formal weddings and 33 percent of brides between 26 and 35).

- ❦ Because approximately 30 percent of all marriages are now second marriages, more children from previous marriages are being included in the ceremony, as well as in the wedding vows.

- ❦ Older brides: in 1950 the average age of brides was 18; today the average age of all brides is 28.6, and the average age of first-time brides is 23.9.

- ❦ Older grooms: the average age of all grooms is 31.2, and the average age of first-time grooms is 26.1.

- ❦ Doing away with receiving lines.

By the way, when it comes to selecting your ceremony site and planning the service itself, here are four new cost-cutting ceremony trends:

- ❦ Marrying at a simple civil ceremony at the county courthouse with only your attendants as witnesses, followed immediately by a large formal reception. This means you don't have to rent or decorate a sanctuary or formal ceremony site and you won't need to provide transportation for the wedding party from the ceremony to the reception.

- ❦ Marrying at the reception site itself. Many brides and grooms are choosing to marry indoors in front of their guests (who may be sitting at tables or standing), or on the patio or in the garden of the reception site. This concept worked well, in fact, for our son and his bride when they were married on the flagstone veranda off their reception hall at The Lodge at Pebble Beach in Carmel, California. The veranda was already included in their reception rental fee, so there was no extra cost and it needed no decorations because of the magnificent ocean view.

- ❦ Marrying at your honeymoon destination. This type of wedding is called a *destination wedding, travel wedding* or *honeymoon wedding* and has become very popular because it saves the cost of a full-blown ceremony and reception. Usually, the couple's closest friends, members of their wedding party and members of their *inner family,* pay their own way to the honeymoon location. Contact the bridal consultant at your honeymoon hotel, or call the visitor's bureau at your honeymoon destination to ask for a list of hotels and resorts that offer this service. It will save you thousands of dollars and, when you return from your honeymoon, if your relatives insist on hosting an informal reception—fine. By the way, some of the more popular destinations for honeymoon weddings are Disneyland in California or Disney World in Florida, cruise ships, and most Las Vegas and Hawaiian resorts.

 Marrying at a *surprise ceremony* at a family gathering, such as at Thanksgiving, Christmas, New Year's or a family reunion Fourth of July picnic. One couple pulled this off beautifully by having the bride's parents invite an unusually large crowd of friends and relatives for Thanksgiving dinner, including the groom's immediate family members. About an hour before dinner was served the couple's minister arrived to perform the surprise wedding ceremony, followed by the sumptuous Thanksgiving meal which doubled as their wedding feast. After the meal the couple left on a four-day Thanksgiving holiday honeymoon. What an ingenious idea! Their only expenses were the minister's fee and the costs of feeding a larger-than-normal Thanksgiving crowd, and yet they were surrounded by loving (although astounded!) friends and members of their immediate families.

I am happy to be able to share these new trends with you throughout this book, along with updated prices and helpful suggestions gleaned from recent brides and grooms all over the country.

My best wishes go to you—enjoy the book and happy planning!

1

Guess What? You're It!

(How to Be Your Own Wedding Consultant)

"What are you going to be when you grow up?" Were you ever asked this question? Of course you never dreamed you would become a wedding consultant!

A wedding consultant—also known as a wedding supervisor, wedding coordinator or professional bridal consultant—plans, advises, supervises, assembles information, makes decisions, places orders, delegates, organizes, assists, coordinates and generally provides a shoulder to cry on. This unique person provides varying numbers of services and charges a variety of fees.

Those coordinators provided by a church or synagogue charge a minimal fee of $50 to $150 to help in a very limited way. Usually they meet with the bride and her mother two or three times, help run the rehearsal, and assist on the wedding day. They do not provide the full service of a professional consultant who is in private practice.

Another type of wedding consultant is the employee of a large department store, bridal salon or florist. The good news about these consultants is that their services are free; the bad news is that their advice usually pertains only to the product they are selling.

The third type of consultant is the private-practice professional. I spoke with these consultants all over the country and was surprised to learn of the differences in their fees and services. First of all, only those consultants who belong to the Association of Bridal Consultants are labeled "Professional Bridal Consultants." These people consider themselves to be much more professional than the others, having taken special training and subscribed to an impressive Code of Ethics. These people coordinate *every* wedding service you can imagine, including the limousine service, tux rentals, airplane and hotel reservations and video production. They charge per hour, per service rendered, or up to 15 percent of the total monies expended for the wedding and reception.

They may charge anywhere from $25 to $50 per hour. Some also charge flat fees for performing certain services, such as $50 to help the bride and bridesmaids line up before the wedding, $200 to assist

at the rehearsal and wedding or $50 for one hour of assistance in selecting wedding invitations.

As you can see, you will save a lot of money by serving as your own consultant. But, more important, you will provide the "full service" that the grandest and best, most trained and professional consultants never can because you have something money can't buy—*LOVE!*

Whether you are the mother of the bride, another family member, a friend or the bride herself, relax and enjoy this precious time of planning. All the research has been done for you. Besides providing the normal wedding costs for your part of the country, I will explain ways of cutting these costs through elimination, substitution, help from friends and family and by doing a lot of things yourself.

Staying Organized Is the Key

There are two things I want you to do before you continue reading this book. The first is to take a deep breath and smile. It will all work out fine. Close your eyes and visualize a perfect wedding. Picture the ceremony, the reception, the happy bride and groom. Envision success with every detail. A positive attitude can make the difference between feeling exhausted or elated after it is all over.

The second thing I want you to do is to purchase a planning workbook or the materials to make one yourself. I have authored a planner specifically designed to be used with this book. It is titled *The Big Wedding on a Small Budget Planner and Organizer*. It is for sale at the same place you purchased this book. Or, you may go to the store with this shopping list:

    ❦ A fat three-ring binder

    ❦ Loose-leaf paper

    ❦ Twelve notebook dividers with tabs and pockets

    ❦ Twelve zippered inserts for a three-ring binder

Pick a notebook in a color you love because it will be your constant companion from now until the wedding. This notebook will be used to get organized, and it will be the key to staying calm and within your budget. It will become the indispensable tool in your new role as wedding consultant. Divide this notebook into the following sections:

1. Budget

2. Calendar

3. Ceremony

4. Clothing

5. Flowers

6. Reception

7. Other Food Service

8. Music

9. Decorations

10. Photography and Video

11. Guest and Gift List

12. Incidentals

In addition to its own divider and plastic zippered insert, each of these sections will also need to be filled with a sizable number of loose-leaf pages, and you will find it handy to attach a pen to the notebook in some permanent way.

After you have read this book you will have an idea of what you should be entering in each of the sections in your notebook. Don't be overwhelmed by these preliminary explanations, for it will all become clear to you as you read along. As an example, the first section of the notebook, "The Budget," cannot be used until you have decided on your own personal budget total and allotments for each of the categories within that total. You will reach these decisions by the end of chapter twelve.

Meanwhile, you will need to have your notebook all set up and ready to use. By the time you finish this book you will be the most organized wedding consultant in town.

The Budget

And so, we come to the first section of your notebook. The Budget gets top billing because all your other plans will revolve around the amount of money you decide to spend on the wedding. Of course, after reading this book, you will have a perfect picture of how much you can spend on each category and which money-saving tricks you will decide to use; chapter twelve will help you determine the distribution of your total funds into these categories. Then you will enter these dollar limits boldly and fearlessly, without feeling guilty about the tiny amounts of money you will be spending. Remember: More is *not* always better and you will have an elaborate-looking wedding without having to auction off the family car. I promise!

The first page of The Budget section will give your overall financial picture showing the amount of money you can spend for each category, with the grand total at the bottom. Following this first page will be one page for each of the eleven categories, with the budgeted dollar limit shown clearly at the top of the page. For example, the page in The Budget section of my notebook marked "Music" showed a dollar limit of $185 and then listed the musicians and what each was to be paid.

After bravely entering your dollar limit at the top of each page in this section, you will keep track of your *actual* expenses by recording each and every one. Even the cost of this notebook should be noted on the page marked "Incidentals." You will find that the small costs will add up too fast unless you are careful. That is why many of the money-saving ideas in this book are for the little things. Even borrowing a basket for the flower girl will save the $15 the florist would charge you for it. Eliminating $15 here and $15 there will save you thousands of dollars—you'll see!

The Calendar

This section is the wedding consultant's Bible; it is filled with lists of "to do's"— all those things that need to be done at certain intervals before the wedding. For example, since my daughter's wedding was at Christmastime, we had lists of things to be done in September, October, November, the first and second weeks of December and then daily right up to the wedding day. We will cover the calendar thoroughly in chapter two and I will frequently remind you to write it down in your notebook, unless, of course, you have purchased my *Big Wedding on a Small Budget Planner and Organizer*, which you will be using.

The Ceremony

Here you will want to write down the actual order of the wedding itself, from the prelude music through the recessional. Fill your zippered insert with a copy of the vows, a copy of the program, a sketch of the layout for the wedding site, whether the site be a church, synagogue, park or private club. You can also use the zippered insert to safeguard the minister's or rabbi's business card.

Use the pages of this section to write down the names of all those participating in the wedding—the bridesmaids, groomsmen, ushers, flower girl, ring bearer, candle lighters, sound man, ministers, etc. Note their addresses and telephone numbers; you will need to refer to them often.

Clothing

This will be one of your busiest sections because you, as the consultant, will have so many things to write down and remember. Every item of clothing you or your attendants may possibly purchase needs to be noted, and you should write down the price, and size, as well as the address and telephone number of the store, name of the salesclerk and every other detail you have time to note for each item. You'll find that it's very difficult to remember the exact features of a certain dress or headpiece unless you write them down.

The plastic zippered compartment for this section will be bulging with fabric swatches, ribbon pieces, pictures of wedding and bridesmaids' dresses, price sheets for tuxedo rentals, business cards, brochures, etc. I feel sorry for anyone planning a wedding who doesn't have all this information together in one place. You can't imagine the satisfaction of being able to open your notebook to find a certain name and telephone number, especially when you are in a hurry and don't have time to hunt for it in a drawer somewhere.

When you read chapters three and four on wedding costumes, you will catch on very quickly to the type of information you will need to note in this section of your notebook or the *Big Wedding on a Small Budget Planner and Organizer.*

Flowers

There are many details you will need to note in this section because there are so many ways to cut costs here. Keep a very careful record of everything you price, devoting a full sheet to each florist you contact. Place any brochures or written bids they may give you into the zippered insert, along with business cards, pieces of floral ribbon and samples of colors. Make note of which florists seem easy to work with, as well as any difference in costs between "in-season" and "out-of-season" flowers.

As you learn about the money-saving ideas explained in chapter five, you will need to note the comparative costs of using each of them. This will mean recording even the smallest items that you will need to buy or borrow, such as florist wire, baskets, floral tape or plant hangers. This section will be full of prices and ideas that will help you decide upon your floral budget and which plan is the best to stay within it.

If your wedding is scheduled for summertime, or you live in a warm climate, friends and relatives may offer you flowers or greenery from their yards. Be sure to keep a record of each of these possibilities. Write down what type of flower or greenery they have offered and their addresses and telephone numbers for future reference. You may decide to go this "free florist" route and you need to be able to remember who offered what.

The Reception

Here you will record the costs for all the various food plans. You will want to write down the exact prices quoted from every caterer you contact and whether these prices are "per person" or "per food item." Then, you will need to record any cost-cutting alternative plan that interests you as explained in chapter six.

There are so many ways to save money in this category, without sacrificing an elegant reception, that you will fill your pages with notes and ideas. When you hear what some caterers charge, you will love my money-saving tricks. Carefully save all caterers' brochures and price lists, as well as delicatessen prices and grocery costs, in case you decide to purchase the food yourself.

Wedding cake prices fall into this category, too. Make note of prices and save pictures of various styles of cakes in your zippered insert. (Rental of the hall is covered in chapter ten under "Incidentals.")

Other Food Service

"Other Food Service" includes the rehearsal dinner, the bridesmaids' luncheon, prewedding snacks for the wedding party and food to have around the house for wedding guests who may be staying overnight. Make lists of what you will be providing and the costs. Chapter six will help you with these plans.

Music

In this section you'll record the names, addresses and telephone numbers of everyone who will be performing during the ceremony and reception. Write down the fee that each will charge. The zippered insert is wonderful for keeping copies of the music for the ceremony. You can also use this section to record "must play" music for the reception.

Decorations

This category includes everything you will need to give the wedding and reception sites that certain ambiance. This will probably be another fat section, with lots of prices and ideas. I enjoyed planning this part of my daughter's wedding more than any other—it was the most creative and there were so many ways to save money.

You will also need to write down the names and telephone numbers of everyone who has offered to loan or contribute something toward your decor, whether it be an old-fashioned wrought iron bench to use in the reception hall or pew ribbons you will be sharing with another wedding. If you're using my *Planner and Organizer*, this job will be even easier because there are fill-in-the-blank pages to use for this purpose. You'll be saving samples of everything, including ribbon, crepe paper, balloons, napkins and paper plates.

Photography and Video

This section will also tend to swell with notes. Chapter nine will help you save hundreds of dollars in this category, but, again, you will need to do a lot of pricing. This will mean a full page for each photographer and videographer, with name, address, telephone number and notes.

When you see various photographers' work, you will notice that each has a particular style that will leave you with an impression. Some photographers like to take more close-ups; others prefer outdoor shots. If you plan to hire a professional photographer, be sure to write your impressions of each in your notebook. Do you like the romantic style of one better than another? What do you feel when you look at a certain photographer's work or videographer's videotape? Write these feelings down; they will become invaluable to you later as you make your decision.

The zippered insert, of course, is handy for the photographers' and videographers' brochures, business cards and actual bids. You will also need to devote several sheets in this section to a list of "must" shots for the photographer. We will discuss this list in chapter nine.

Guest and Gift List

This is obviously where you will record the name and address of every person who will receive an invitation. If you ask for an RSVP for the reception, record the response beside each name. In fact, leave four columns to the right of each name and address for:

- ❧ Date Invitation Mailed

- ❧ RSVP Response

- ❧ Description of Gift Received (if any)

- ❧ Date Thank-You Note Mailed

This is a great time-saver when it comes to writing thank-you notes because you will have the mailing addresses and descriptions of the gifts side by side.

Your sheets could look like this:

Name & Address	Invitation Mailed	RSVP	Gift Description	Thank-You Mailed
Suzanne Smith 125 Main St. Modesto, CA 95380	5/20	Yes	Crystal bowl	8/28
Richard and Susan Wilson Box 395 Cripple Creek, CO 80813	5/20	No	Candlesticks	8/28
Blake Evans 2342 Dawn St. Goshen, CA 93227	5/20	Yes	Place setting	8/28

For your convenience, I've included a blank form on the following page that can be photocopied for your notebook.

In addition to this guest/gift list, this section should have a full sheet devoted to each stationer and printer you contact for prices of invitations or announcements. Also, make note of the particular styles and wordings you prefer.

Your zippered section should contain a copy of the invitation or announcement you finally select.

Incidentals

Here you should include such things as the marriage license, blood tests, hair appointments, postage and other little things that don't seem to fit into any of the main categories. We will discuss all these pesky details in chapter ten, but this is the section of your notebook for keeping track of them.

Don't forget that the *actual* expenses for all the categories are to be recorded in the first section of your notebook on the appropriate page in your Budget section.

Whether you purchase the *Big Wedding on a Small Budget Planner and Organizer* or create your own notebook, you need to get excited about using it. If you are an organized person, this will be great fun for you. If you are not, try to be organized

Name & Address	Invitation Mailed	RSVP	Gift Description	Thank-You Mailed

just this one time in your life. You might like it. You might like it so much, in fact, that you will take up a new career after the wedding is over—that of a professional wedding consultant.

The main thing to remember is you must get this notebook set up right away and *use it daily*. It will keep you calm and in control. And, most important, it will *keep you within your budget*. You will find when it is all over that you had a much more elaborate wedding than you ever thought you could afford.

Acting as your own wedding consultant, you'll feel sorry for those unfortunate people who let the wedding plan them, instead of vice versa. They spend money as they go, getting caught up in the emotion of the moment. They also let themselves be put on a guilt trip. A photographer, for example, may give them a sales pitch that plays on their emotions with the phrase, "This is a once-in-a-lifetime decision . . . you'll be sorry later if you don't spend more now." Things get out of control and when those who don't plan get close to the wedding date, they often realize they are running out of money. Panic sets in; they may frantically borrow against their Visa or MasterCard. Some even put second mortgages on their homes.

But I know this won't happen to you because, after reading this book, you will have hundreds of ways to save money, and a notebook to keep you on track.

After your wedding is over, by the way, you will probably find that your notebook will become very popular. Mine did. Many of my friends were planning weddings and asked to borrow it. I always said "yes," although my heart was in my mouth—what if they lost it? I not only needed it to write this book, but it has sentimental value to our family. It is full of memories—of the details and the fun we had planning. I shouldn't have worried, however, for my friends always returned it in its original bulging condition, no worse for the wear. And they all saved money by using my ideas.

Don't forget that, as the efficient wedding consultant, you must keep this notebook with you at all times between now and the wedding. You never know when you will need it because you tend to find bargain items where you least expect them.

My notebook was locked in the trunk of my car whenever I was away from home. Once when I was out shopping for something else I came across a bin of ribbon on sale. Some of the rolls seemed to be the right shade of burgundy, but I wasn't sure, so I ran to the car to grab a color sample out of my notebook. The sale ribbon was perfect and I made the purchase.

I also found treasures at garage sales and, again, it was handy to have the notebook with me. It was at a garage sale, in fact, that I found the burgundy silk flowers I used to make the bridesmaids' headpieces.

The notebook was with me to the end. I almost decided to leave it home on the day of the wedding—after all, the planning was done. But I hauled it with me anyway, and am I glad I did!

Right at the last minute my daughter panicked. It was almost time for her to walk down the aisle and she couldn't remember the wedding vows. She said, "Mom, read me the vows—quick! My mind has gone blank!"

I picked up the notebook, turned to the Ceremony section and took a copy of the vows out of the zippered insert. I read the vows to her, just like the minister would do, and she repeated them to me. This calmed her down and during the ceremony she said the vows clearly and without hesitation.

My notebook was a good friend and I was so glad I had it with me when Lynn panicked that I even gave it a little hug. Then I looked around, hoping no one had seen me, for surely people would say, "Look, the poor dear has gone bonkers. This wedding sent her right over the edge."

You'll probably hug your notebook from time to time, too, but that will be our little secret—I'll never tell if you don't!

Acting as your own wedding consultant will not only provide you with a creative and satisfying "new career," but will save you a lot of money! As you march off, notebook under your arm, just keep repeating one thing over and over: "I'm saving thousands of dollars . . . I'm saving thousands of dollars. . . ."

So, take a deep breath, picture a perfect wedding, and don't forget to smile. You're in for one of the most creative, satisfying times of your life!

2

Dream It Up
and Write It Down

(Preplanning and the Calendar)

Isn't your notebook beautiful? I'm so proud of you—you're on the path to organization and control! As you noticed, the second section of your notebook is called the "Calendar." This section will contain pages of planning notes, from general to specific. Your preplanning ideas should come first, followed by a very detailed and complete calendar. Think of your preplanning as a broad road and your calendar as little side streets. You must be on the right road or you will never find the side streets; that's why you need to do some preplanning so that you will be headed in the right direction.

Preplanning

This stage of your life should be the time when you can sit back in your favorite chair and do a little "right-brain thinking" before we get down to the calendar itself, which by its very nature must be hard and disciplined. We will get to that taskmaster later in this chapter, but for now, let your mind ponder the big picture. Let it ask questions, such as:

- ❦ What is my vision of the ideal ceremony?

- ❦ What kind of theme would be nice for the reception?

- ❦ What colors do I like?

- ❦ What month would be best for the wedding?

- ❦ Do I want to get married out-of-doors?

- ❦ How big should the wedding be?

🐦 Who should I invite? What about out-of-town guests?

🐦 What role will my future in-laws take in the proceedings?

🐦 Who should I ask to be my maid of honor?

🐦 Will my sister (best friend, cousin) help me with the wedding?

These are some of the things to consider during this preplanning stage. Don't take off running before you're on the right road—that would be a tragic waste of time. Take it slow and enjoy! This may be your only "dreamin' time" between now and the wedding—use it wisely. By the way, dream with the notebook open, for the first pages of the calendar section should be filled with these brainstorming notes.

Visualize Your Ideal Wedding

If money weren't a problem at all, what kind of a wedding would you want? Think back to weddings you've attended. What struck you about them? What stands out in your memory? What touched your heart? Write these things down as you remember them. They may not be as impossible to incorporate into your own wedding as you may think.

How do you want the guests to feel at your wedding? What kind of music do you want played? Can you picture the flowers? What are they? Roses? Close your eyes— can you smell their fragrance right now?

What about your dress? Do you like the drop-waist look that is so royally elegant? Or do you prefer the fresh and innocent look of puffed sleeves and eyelet lace? Can you picture yourself in one of those sleek, contemporary dresses with the asymmetrical headpiece? Don't be afraid to drool over Lady Diana's dress either, because, although you won't be able to buy a dress like hers, you may be able to rent one that comes very close. Don't limit your imagination. By the time you get to chapter three, these dreams may become possible by using one of our magic cost-cutting plans. Look through bridal magazines and see if you begin to sense a mood, a feeling—yes, even a theme for your wedding.

Themes will be covered in chapter eight, but you should be thinking about them now. There are traditional themes, such as Hearts and Flowers, Cupid and Love Doves, or Winter Wonderland. Some of the nontraditional party themes for the reception include Polynesian, the fifties, the Roaring twenties, or a Ship's Cruise. The theme for the wedding should be fairly traditional, but the trend for the reception has been to toss out the old ideas and bring in the new. Let your mind settle on that thought for a moment and if any ideas come drifting by, grab them and capture them in your notebook; they might be very useful when you come to chapter eight.

One thing you will find as you read this book is that a wedding is a lot like a play or theatrical event, performed on a beautiful stage created by illusion and suggestion. The audience, or wedding guests, don't notice that the "sets" are fabricated, because the overall effect is magnificent. I will teach you how to work this magic so that your wedding day will seem out of this world. Meanwhile, let your dreams take over, for anything is possible.

Now, close your eyes and listen for a moment. What do you hear? Violins? A harp? The magnificent strains of an organ? A gentle piano? Before everyone begins offering you advice on who should sing at your wedding, or who is a good pianist or flautist, set up some priorities in your own mind. Do you want a quiet, classical kind of wedding and reception with soft piano music? Or, how about the tender sounds of a guitar? These are thoughts to ponder. Don't make a decision today, but become aware of the possibilities. Write down your impressions in your notebook. Be ready for the decisions when they need to be made in chapter seven.

When you walk into the reception on the arm of your new husband, what do you see on the buffet table? Finger sandwiches? French pastries? Jot down the yummy things you envision at your reception. Picture the guests as they celebrate with you.

By the way, what colors did you see in the reception? Pink? Mint green? Robin's egg blue? Yes, you will need to decide on a color scheme that will be carried throughout your wedding and reception. What colors have you seen at recent weddings you've attended? Is there a color that is very special to you? One that makes you feel joyous and uplifted? Jot it down in your notebook and watch for color samples the next time you are out and about.

Where would you like to get married? In a church? Beside a roaring surf? In a rose garden? Don't let anyone pressure you into getting married in a building if you dream of getting married outdoors. If you want ideas for outdoor sites, contact your area Chamber of Commerce, parks commission, historical society or the National Register of Historic Trusts. There is also a nationwide directory called *Places* (get it at your library). Many of these sites rent quite reasonably; for example, the Rose Garden at Golden Gate Park in San Francisco is available for weddings at $125 for the first two hours and includes the use of the adjacent park for the reception at $75 for all day, and—the best news of all—these rates are the same for residents and nonresidents alike. So, don't let tradition bind you; have your wedding wherever you want. It is your dream.

How about the ceremony itself? Have you always wanted to write your own vows? Ask your clergyman about this idea; it is entirely possible. Many couples are composing their entire ceremonies, as well as their vows.

If you would like to write your own vows, I have written a new book that may be helpful entitled *Diane Warner's Complete Book of Wedding Vows* that offers over three hundred vow phrasings, from contemporary to classical.

Picture the wedding party, your handsome groom, his smiling mother. In fact, picture a perfect day in every way—the kind of ideal wedding day you have always dreamed of having. The experts say that you can make things happen by creating a positive image in your mind, so visualize perfection in every detail, and your dreams will come true.

A Little Wedding Etiquette

At an exciting time like this, who wants a lesson in manners? I admit this doesn't sound like the most interesting of topics, and I hate to wake you so abruptly from your dreams, but a certain amount of the preplanning has to do with etiquette.

It is impossible for me to cover everything you need to know on this subject because it would fill an entire book; however, I will touch on a couple of things that pertain to preplanning, and you can read the rest in a good wedding etiquette book. I recommend *Emily Post's Complete Book of Wedding Etiquette*, by Elizabeth L. Post, available in your local library. It will answer hundreds of questions, such as "Where do I seat the bride's divorced grandparents and their new spouses?" This is a touchy question, and obviously needs an answer from Ms. Post.

Meanwhile, your most immediate planning should involve a meeting with your future in-laws. It is a good idea for the bride, groom and both sets of parents to sit down and discuss who will pay for what part of the wedding festivities. The rehearsal dinner, for example, is usually provided by the groom's parents, who may also want to help with some of the reception costs. Of course, in the case where the bride and groom are footing all the bills, it isn't necessary to discuss expenses with the parents, but it's always considered proper etiquette to arrange an introductory meeting between them so they feel included in the plans.

It's also not too soon to discuss hotel or motel accommodations for the days of the rehearsal and wedding; usually the parents of the groom agree to pay for their own accommodations, but the parents of the bride offer to arrange them. Of course, if everyone lives close by, this isn't a problem.

At this time, it's also a good idea to discuss the guest list. The groom and his parents should provide the bride and her family with their list so that the correct number of invitations can be ordered as soon as possible. Invitations should be addressed and ready to mail six to eight weeks before the wedding, and they take about a month to have printed.

Don't be afraid to bring your notebook to this meeting; as all these decisions are made, especially regarding the plans for the rehearsal dinner, make notes in the proper sections of your notebook. Anything regarding the rehearsal dinner should be noted in section seven and decisions regarding the accommodations should be entered in section twelve.

You aren't the only one who needs to know about wedding etiquette; others in the wedding party are also expected to behave in a certain way. Whether they will or not remains to be seen, but this is what is expected.

Best Man

The best man is an all-purpose kind of guy. He has many responsibilities. In general, he must see that everything runs smoothly. He encourages the groom when he feels stressed; makes all the bride and groom's travel arrangements; supervises the ushers; serves as an official witness to the vows; safeguards the rings and marriage license; pays the clergyman's fee; and proposes a toast at the bridal table. He also returns all the rented tuxes. His final duty is to be sure the wedding party lines up properly for the "wedding parade" through town.

Maid or Matron of Honor

She is the one the bride turns to for help. She helps address invitations and records who sends gifts. On the actual wedding day she has many duties: she distributes all corsages and boutonnieres; helps dress the bride and bridesmaids; holds the bride's bouquet and the groom's ring during the ceremony; serves as an official witness to the vows; arranges the bride's train during the ceremony; helps the bride change into her going-away outfit; and collects the bride's attire for safekeeping.

Groomsmen

The groomsmen are very important members of the wedding party, for they make the first impression on the guests as they arrive; they greet the guests and seat them on the proper side of the church. Immediately before the ceremony two of the groomsmen seat the groom's mother and then the bride's mother; after the ceremony they escort them down the aisle. Groomsmen should be available to assist the bride's mother at any time with last-minute details and they should add to the festivity of the reception by introducing guests to each other. The other major duty of the groomsmen is to arrange transportation of the bridesmaids to the wedding site. By the way, although groomsmen usually do double-duty, also serving as ushers before the ceremony begins, in many cases there are two sets of men: groomsmen *and* ushers. In this case, the ushers seat the guests.

Bridesmaids

The bridesmaids should be called upon to help the bride at any time before the wedding. They can help make wedding favors and run errands for the bride or her mother during the last week. They have no official responsibilities on the wedding day other than to look pretty and add to the festive spirit.

The Calendar

This brings us to our lifesaver—the calendar. Don't you feel sorry for those poor people who are trying to plan a wedding without a timetable? You will learn to depend on your calendar and it will let you know where you stand at any moment. Set up one page in your calendar section for each month before the wedding. Then set up a separate page for each of the three weeks before the big day. The last few days before the wedding will be filled with intricate details and you will need a full page for each one.

It is ideal to have a year to plan a wedding; however, six months can be plenty of time. If you only have three or four months, it can still be done, but you will feel a little more rushed because you will be cramming all the "As Soon as Possible" duties into one month's time. Also, you may have to take second or third choice of florist, caterer, minister, musicians and photographer. Your wedding dress may have to be sewn or bought off the rack. Our daughter, for instance, bought her dress one afternoon and walked out of the shop with it in her arms. It happened to fit perfectly and she could have been married in it that evening if necessary.

We planned our daughter's wedding with only four months' notice and we were very fortunate that we only had to take second choice in one category—the caterer. But we were very pleased with our second choice and it probably worked out for the best anyway. When I look back on it now, the main disadvantage of this tight time schedule was the lack of "dreamin' time" as I described earlier in this chapter. We couldn't afford that luxury. As soon as the engagement was announced, my daughter and I hit the ground running and never stopped right up to the wedding day. If we would have even had six months, it would have been a great help. But at least we proved it can be done, and done right, in only four months.

Here are the recommended duties to be entered on your calendar; copy them onto your calendar pages. Then, as each duty is completed, check it off with a big fat felt-tip pen!

Wedding Calendar: What to Do When

As Soon as Possible

❦ Select the date and time of the wedding. (Be sure to read chapter six before deciding on a time.)

❦ Reserve the wedding and reception sites.

❦ Choose the members of the wedding party.

❦ Decide on the color scheme.

❦ Set a firm budget; put it in your notebook's Budget section.

❦ Meet with the parents of the groom.

❦ Make an appointment with the clergyman or rabbi.

❦ Start the guest list.

❦ Begin planning the reception.

❦ Select the wedding dress.

❦ Choose mothers' dresses.

- ❦ Select the attendants' dresses.

- ❦ Arrange for the junior attendants' attire.

- ❦ Decide on the theme (see chapter eight).

Four Months Before the Wedding

- ❦ Finalize plans for the reception: refreshments; decorations; favors; etc. Note which things can be assembled ahead of time by friends and family who have volunteered to help.

- ❦ Complete guest lists.

- ❦ Order invitations, thank-you notes and napkins.

- ❦ Order the wedding cake.

- ❦ Select a photography/videography plan.

- ❦ Select a floral plan.

- ❦ Select a music plan.

- ❦ Select the food plan and begin baking and preparing foods that can be frozen ahead of time, if necessary.

- ❦ Decide on your decorations.

- ❦ Engage volunteers to help with reception, flowers, photography, music, decorations and any other items. Write down their names in your notebook. Designate supervisors for each category.

Three Months Before the Wedding

- ❦ Plan the ceremony, including the writing of your own vows, if desired.

- ❦ Reserve the rental of the men's wedding attire.

- ❦ Schedule a medical appointment for blood tests at least a month before the wedding day.

- ❦ Begin addressing invitations.

Two Months Before the Wedding

- Purchase or borrow the small items, such as the ring pillow, garter, guest book, etc.

- Make up the list of "must" photography and videography shots.

- Arrange for the rental of certain items that are part of your cost-cutting plans.

- Mail the invitations.

- Begin writing thank-you notes for any shower or engagement gifts received to date.

- Select the specific music to be performed during the ceremony and reception.

One Month Before the Wedding

- Apply for the marriage license.

- Keep the medical appointment for blood tests.

- Send a wedding announcement to the local newspaper.

- Plan the bridesmaids' luncheon.

- Schedule final fitting for wedding dress.

- Coordinate the rehearsal dinner.

- Have final meetings with the florist, caterer, photographer and musicians, or the volunteers helping on one of the cost-cutting plans.

- Arrange accommodations for out-of-town guests.

Three Weeks Before the Wedding

- Arrange for all the men renting tuxedos to be measured at the rental shop.

- Finalize rehearsal details.

❧ Arrange transportation for the wedding party to and from the church and reception.

Two Weeks Before the Wedding

❧ Confirm the reception guest list and inform the caterer of the number.

❧ Pack for the honeymoon.

❧ Deliver list of "must" shots to the photographer and videographer.

❧ Hire nursery workers to care for small children, if necessary.

❧ Make out a seating plan and place cards for the rehearsal dinner.

❧ Arrange for the transport of your gifts to your home on the wedding day.

One Week Before the Wedding

❧ Make up and mail a time schedule to everyone involved in the wedding.

❧ Confirm one last time with the florist, caterer, photographer, etc.

❧ Have final fitting of the wedding gown.

❧ Attend the bridesmaids' luncheon.

❧ Confirm rehearsal plans with the clergy.

❧ Pack boxes of supplies for the rehearsal, wedding and reception.

Daily During the Week Before the Wedding

You will have daily lists of things to do that are unique to your own wedding. My family teased me because of my detailed lists. Whatever I didn't get done one day, I transferred to the next until there was no time left. The only major thing we forgot was the marriage license. It should have been given to the minister ahead of time, but a half hour before the wedding was to begin, the minister came to me and asked for it; I said that I didn't know where it was—I thought the groom was responsible for it. Well, it turned out that the groom had given it to our daughter, who put it on her dresser for safekeeping. The minister refused to marry them without it. So my husband drove home, found it among her things and returned just in the nick of time. Everything came off on schedule, and no one ever knew of the temporary crisis. The lesson to be learned from this is that, as wedding coordinator, you need to follow up on everything. Don't assume anyone will remember anything, even if it does make you feel like a drill sergeant at times.

There is one very important thing for you to remember: You won't have to do it all alone—learn to delegate! You will have dozens of friends and relatives who will ask if there is anything they can do to help. After reading this book, you will not only have cost-cutting plans for staying on your budget, but a nice fat list of things for your volunteers to do as well.

If your "wedding consultant hat" is feeling awfully tight about now, take it off for a moment and relax. I wore that same hat, so I know the overwhelming responsibility you feel but, trust me, the fear will disappear as you get used to your new role. Your anxiety will be replaced by warm feelings of satisfaction as you see the results of your planning.

3
She'll Wear Satins and Laces . . .

(Become a Cinderella Without a Fairy Godmother)

You have your notebook open and ready and your calendar is by your side. All you need is something to coordinate. How about the purchase of the wedding gown? After all, the wedding is six months away, and it is time to make this important decision! You will find as you do your planning that nothing compares with the excitement of selecting the bride's attire. When other subjects are discussed, such as the photography, flowers or filling the guests' tummies with food, the bride will smile politely and offer her suggestions. But when we talk about her dress, she sits up straight, her eyes sparkle and her attention span increases dramatically.

The wedding guests are interested in her dress, too. You rarely hear a guest asking, "What are they serving at the reception?" or "What kind of flowers did they choose for the chapel?" The questions most asked before the wedding are: "Have you seen her dress?" "How long is the train?" "What does it look like?" "Has the groom seen it yet?"

On her wedding day the bride becomes the center of attention, and that is why her dress is the most important purchase. But, it doesn't need to be an expensive one to be memorable.

In this chapter I will give you some good ways to cut your costs on all the bridal accoutrements, and you can do so without sacrificing style or quality. You are probably worried that I plan to drape the bride with lace tablecloths, or something equally tacky, but dismiss such horrible thoughts from your mind! I promise that your bride will be the envy of Lady Di as she glides down the aisle in her exquisite dress.

The worst thing you can do is what my daughter and I did: we bought her dress at a bridal salon! This is the most expensive way to go but, unfortunately, I did not have a book like this one to explain the cost-cutting alternatives.

When our daughter became engaged, her first reaction was to try on dresses. We bought bridal magazines and drooled over the gorgeous styles. There were stacks of these magazines on our coffee table with dog-eared pages marking her favorite dresses. It was such fun to ponder the choices, while leisurely nursing a hot cup of coffee. This was followed by many trips to bridal salons where she tried on six or eight dresses each time. Some styles were more flattering than others, and we made note of the particular dresses that were possibilities.

We also hounded the bridal salons in the finer department stores. It took a month of looking before our daughter found the perfect dress. It happened quite unexpectedly, in fact. One day we asked my mother-in-law to go dress shopping with us. We thought this would be fun for her, and since she was in poor health, we selected a small bridal salon close to her home. We did not expect to find the right dress in such a small shop, but since we were going there for Grandma's benefit, it didn't really matter. Of course, that is the very shop that had the perfect dress. We bought the dress right off the rack, plus the headpiece and veil, and slip, and later purchased some satin slippers.

This is what we spent that day:

Wedding dress	$400
Headpiece and veil	$120
Petticoat	$ 50
Total	$570

There is an interesting fact about some bridal salons: Most of the sales staff are on commission and will try to sell you a dress whether it is right or not. One of the things, in fact, that bothered me the most about sales personnel we encountered was the way they praised every dress my daughter tried on. It became very annoying.

Another problem with these shops is that they ask for your name, address, telephone number, time and place of the wedding and some use this information for profit by *selling* it to florists, caterers, photographers and consultants. These pushy people will call you, usually during the dinner hour, not only robbing you of precious time, but exerting sales pressure. It is a lot like inviting a vacuum cleaner salesman into your living room—not much fun!

Another complaint I've heard about bridal salons is that they often encourage the bride, and other members of the bridal party, to order larger sizes than they need. They want to be able to charge you to alter the dress to the proper size after it comes in. In fact, it has been said that bridal salons make as much off their alterations as they do the sales themselves. Several bridal salons I checked have bridal alterations *starting* at $200! So, beware of this ploy! Ask to see the manufacturer's sizing chart and use your own judgment when ordering a bridal gown.

In spite of all this, if you still decide to go through a bridal salon, just remember that it is *your* wedding—you are in charge. Don't let the salesperson control you.

However, I must say in all fairness to the thousands of honest, ethical bridal consultants and owners of bridal salons throughout the country, that not all consultants and salespeople fall into this category, of course. Much of the mail I have received in response to this book has been from honest people in the field, including one from Terrilynn Voisin which read: "The impression you give of bridal consultants paints a very frightening picture, and I take great offense to that. . . . As for myself, I have always been honest with my clients. If a particular dress does not look flattering on the customer, I would gladly lose a sale than sell her something she will not be happy with. . . . I admit there are bridal salons out there that give the whole industry a bad name, but I do not consider us one of them. We serve our brides and do it to the best of our ability. . . ."

I know there are many people out there in the wedding industry who give this kind of honest service, and my best advice to you, my readers, is to talk to other brides and ask them for references before patronizing a bridal salon.

If you choose to purchase your gown from one of these salons, here is what you can expect to pay for a gown in your part of the country:

AREA	COST
Northeastern States—Metropolitan	$1,300
Northeastern States	$1,200
Southeastern States	$1,000
Midwestern States	$ 650
Central Mountain States	$ 800
Northwestern States	$1,000
Southwestern States	$1,100
California—Metropolitan	$1,400
California	$ 800

These prices do not include the headpiece and veil, shoes or petticoat. The headpieces and veils start at about $100, the shoes around $40 and petticoats $75.

Now that we have thoroughly depressed ourselves with these figures, let's move on to the good news! I have eight cost-cutting ideas for you.

Prices in each plan are for the wedding dress only; cost-cutting ideas for the headpiece, veil, petticoat and shoes are given later in this chapter.

The Bride's Dress

Something Borrowed
Approximate Cost. $50

The total cost for this plan is the price of an alteration, if it is required. The dress may be one you have borrowed from a friend, or it may be a family heirloom.

If you borrow a dress from a friend, be sure she has been married for at least a year. She deserves to feel like Cinderella for the first year and really shouldn't loan out her dress. After a year, of course, she feels like an "old married lady" and is glad to share her dress with a friend. It is very important, by the way, to have the dress altered back to its original size after you have worn it. This can be done by recording the exact measurement a seam is taken in or let out. A large stitch (size 7) is preferable to avoid seam marks.

In the case of an older wedding dress that belongs to the bride's mother, grandmother or other relative, it will probably need to be mended or dry-cleaned before it can be worn.

In any case, if you borrow your wedding dress, be sure to have it dry-cleaned before returning it.

Rent It
Approximate Cost. . . . . $100 and up

If I knew then what I know now, this is the idea I would encourage. When our daughter planned her wedding, I didn't know you could rent wedding dresses. Since that time, however, I have seen so many breathtakingly expensive dresses that have been rented, I feel this is the obvious choice. By the way, these dresses can usually be altered.

You can spend up to $350 if you want to rent a more expensive dress. A rental company in Seattle, for example, advertises that their $350 rental dress "retails for $1,000." It is not necessary to go this high, however, as the lower-priced rentals are for wedding gowns that would normally retail from $500 to $700.

One rental shop, for example, Island Bridal Gown Rentals in Hicksville, New York, has gown rentals starting at $100, with over five hundred gowns in stock ranging in size from 4 to 22. There are also national mail-order rental companies, two of which are Tux Town and Classic Collection in Bountiful, Utah (800) 824-0047, and Jandy Rentals in Knoxville, Tennessee (800) 342-1544.

Rental prices vary from shop to shop throughout the country. The main problem you will have is finding a good shop close enough to your hometown. All the larger cities seem to have wedding attire for rent, and many of the smaller cities do, too, but you may have to drive thirty or forty minutes to find what you want. These rental stores can be found in the Yellow Pages under:

❦ Bridal Attire

❦ Costumes

❦ Wedding Rentals

❦ Rentals

"Prom It"
Approximate Cost. *$100*

Have you noticed prom dresses lately? Many are back to the fifties look with the bouffant skirt. If you shop carefully, you will find that some of these dresses can easily be embellished into a wedding dress. If it is a strapless gown, just add detached puffed sleeves and a train made out of the same type fabric or lace. The train can be attached to the top of the bodice or at the waist. Make it detachable so it can be removed during the reception. When you are shopping for matching fabric, be sure you have the dress with you. If you doubt your own talents as a seamstress, you may want to have this done by a professional.

You should also look in the "after-five" or evening wear sections of your local department store. There are some very sleek and contemporary dresses available here that can be embellished with a train for a sophisticated look.

For example, a recent twenty-seven-year-old bride in Chicago found her wedding dress on the sale rack at Lord & Taylor: an $80 white lace cocktail dress which she remodeled only slightly by removing what she called a "really ugly rhinestone pin" and a "fake chiffon overskirt," resulting in a sleek, sleeveless lace sheath.

Some cities have factory outlet stores; try them for prom dresses or evening wear that can be converted to wedding gowns. San Francisco, for example, is loaded with these stores and is known especially for its Gunne Sax outlet. Outlet stores offer prices up to 80 percent off regular retail, especially JCPenney Outlet Stores, if you happen to have one near you.

Another source of suitable dresses is the antique store. Very often you will find an old-fashioned Victorian-style dress for sale alongside an antique chest or brass bed. And don't rule out flea markets, as unlikely as that seems. I have often found white evening dresses for sale at such places; they are even wrapped in their original plastic, having been worn only once.

The main thing is to keep an open mind. By embellishing an existing dress, you can have an absolutely unique creation.

Bridesmaid's Gown in White
Approximate Cost. *$120*

Something the bridal shop staff won't tell you is that many brides purchase their dresses from the bridesmaids' rack. Bridesmaids' dresses are often available in white or ivory and are considerably less expensive than the bridal gown. Some of the dresses even have a train, but if you want a longer one, just add it yourself.

The Distress Sale Dress
Approximate Cost. *$100*

This is a sad thought, but sometimes a wedding dress is bought and never worn. Maybe the bride found out that her prince was right out of the Arabian Nights—you know, the one with a harem. Or, perhaps, that his "rewarding career in the aluminum business" turned out to be collecting empty pop cans from trash bins. In any case, her loss might be your gain.

Here are some recent ads from the classified section of local newspapers:

"Wedding dress, never worn, size 14, originally $450, sacrifice at $100"

"Wedding gown, special order designer gown, size 10, originally $1,200, asking $350"

"Wedding dress, new, $150"

Take a look at some of these dresses; try them on. If the dress seems right, make an offer. In fact, make a low offer. Usually, the owner is delighted to get rid of it.

Free Seamstress
Approximate Cost. $195

If you're handy, why not purchase the pattern and fabric and sew the dress yourself? Or you may have a talented aunt or grandmother who would be honored to sew the dress for you. There are many advantages to making your own dress:

- You can try on wedding dresses in salons to find a style that is becoming, then buy a similar pattern.

- The dress will fit you perfectly.

- You know the dress will be ready for the wedding.

- It will cost you a fraction of the price of a store-bought dress.

More brides would make their own wedding dresses if they only realized one thing: There is no need to worry about ruining the fabric! Do what the professional seamstress does: make it first out of an old sheet. You don't need to make the entire dress, only the bodice and sleeves. And this preliminary sewing job doesn't have to be neat and tidy either. It just has to give you an idea of the style and fit. If the bride doesn't like her "sheet version," ditch the pattern and buy another one. There are dozens to choose from.

Considering the money that will be saved by making your own dress, what is a little money spent on a few patterns? Try them out, just like you would try on a finished dress. Then, when you have a bodice that fits and flatters, lay it out on the fabric and cut away. The fear is gone—you know the dress will turn out right.

Here are all the costs to sew a typical pattern. The price of the pattern is $20 and it includes two versions of a wedding gown and a coordinating bridesmaid's gown. The wedding dress has long sleeves and an average-length train.

MATERIALS	COST
Pattern	$ 20.00
Fabric, 9¾ yards of 45″ taffeta @ $5.99 per yard	58.40
Lining, 9 yards of 45″ acetate @ $4.49 per yard	40.41
Lace for overbodice and sleeves, 1¾ yards, 45″ @ $6.99 per yard	12.23
Tulle for overbodice and sleeves, 1½ yards, 54″ @ $2.98 per yard	4.47
Alençon Galloon lace, 6¾ yards at 4¾″ wide @ $5.99 per yard	40.43
Thread	1.85
Two ⅜″ buttons for sleeves @ $.50 each	1.00
One package soutache braid for button loops	1.89
Zipper, 18″	2.60
800 sequins in one package	1.00
200 small pearls in one package	1.25
Aleene's "No-Sew" Fabric Glue, one bottle	2.39
Twenty satin-covered buttons @ $.40 each	8.00
Total	$195.92

The prices of these materials are straight out of a local fabric store in the small town where I live. None of the fabrics were on sale. If you have the time to shop for bargains or if you are willing to make the dress from less expensive fabrics, the total cost can be cut by at least another 25 percent. I took these prices just as I found them so you know how easy it is to walk into any fabric store and buy what you need.

The mysterious-sounding items called for on the pattern, such as the Alençon Galloon lace or the soutache braid looping, are available in any fabric store. Just ask the sales staff for help—they know where everything is located.

The pearls and sequins, also listed on the pattern, can be glued onto the dress. They go on easily with "No-Sew" glue or a hot-glue gun. The pearls, sequins and glue are found in the craft section of the store.

Just remember that you should not purchase any fabric until you have made the pattern up in sheeting first. When you are sure you will like the dress, go back to the fabric store to purchase your materials.

Hire a Seamstress
Approximate Cost *$321*

Take the same dress described under the "Free Seamstress" plan and hire a seam-stress to sew it for you. I had a Simplicity pattern priced out for me by various seam-stresses, and the labor came to approximately $125. The materials and labor together would total under $321. Many of the seamstresses I spoke with will help the bride shop for the pattern and fabric. They will also come to the wedding with their portable sewing kits in hand to do any last-minute alterations. Some will even shorten or lengthen sleeves on the men's tuxes, replace a button or shorten a hem at the last minute. Most do not charge for this service if they have been hired to sew the clothes for the entire wedding party.

By the way, the one fabric they all seem to advise against is genuine silk. They say it is too difficult to work with, even for the professionals. There are many synthetic "silks" that are just as lovely as the real thing.

These are some of the advantages of this "Hire a Seamstress" plan:

- ❦ The dress will be well made and will fit exactly right.

- ❦ There will be much less stress on the bride and her mother.

- ❦ It may prevent friction within the family just in case a well-meaning relative does a poor job.

Buy from a Resale Shop
Approximate Cost . . . . *50%–75% off Retail*

Resale and consignment shops have always done a big business in this country but, due to our recent recession, they have flourished. Some of these shops sell all kinds of clothes, some only women's clothes, and some specialize in wedding attire. A typical example is Vows Resale Bridal Boutique, located in Newton, Massachusetts, which specializes in "once-worn" and "never-worn" discontinued designer gowns at greatly discounted prices. This particular store always has at least two hundred gowns to choose from, but the shops in your home state may offer even more than that. Look in your yellow pages and give these stores a chance; you may find just the perfect gown without a four to six month ordering delay—you can take the gown home with you the same day.

Buy Discount
Approximate Cost . . . . *$50–$450*

The discount market is everywhere, including factory outlet stores and through cata-logs. The Gunne Sax factory outlet in San Francisco, for example, has a separate building just for the sale of wedding attire. Their selection is especially suitable for the bride who loves the Victorian look. There are other discount stores all over the country including special discount bridal salons and department store outlets. Check your Yellow Pages under "Bridal" for possibilities. Also, check the Yellow Pages under "Department Stores" for outlets in your area.

Another source of discounted bridal gowns is the bridal salon itself; they often offer their "sample" gowns on a special rack, discounted from 25 to 50 percent. Of course you have to luck out with the fit.

One of the easiest ways to buy discount is through a discount broker. Yes, there are discount brokers who specialize in bridal attire. One of the best is Discount Bridal Service who has over a hundred representatives throughout the country. They can offer you name brand dresses at 20 to 40 percent off the retail prices. Here is DBS's toll-free number: (800)874-8794. They will put you in touch with their representative in your area.

The current JCPenney bridal catalog has wedding dresses that range from $175 to $495. If you are turned off by the idea of buying a wedding gown from JCPenney, you probably haven't shopped there lately. But don't be guilty of having even less sense than money, for they sell some of the exact same dresses that are for sale in bridal salons at much higher prices.

The Bridal Suit
Approximate Cost. *$150*

It has become very fashionable the past couple of years for the bride to wear a white or ivory suit. This idea will save you hundreds of dollars; you can find one in the "After-Five" or "Finer Dress" sections of your favorite department store.

The Bride's Headpiece

If you decide to purchase the headpiece and veil from a bridal salon, you will pay between $100 and $350. There is a terrific markup on these items. But, like the wedding dress, there are several ways to save money.

Just remember that whether you buy or make the headpiece, it should coordinate with the dress. Also, the length of the veil depends on the formality of the dress and the wedding itself. If the dress is street-length, the veil should be shorter. If the dress is floor-length and the wedding is formal, the veil should be fingertip length. For a more informal wedding, the bride may wish to dispense with a veil altogether and wear only a hat or flower in her hair.

Also, be sure the headpiece and veil are compatible with the dress. Don't match up an exotic space-age headpiece with a ruffly "Southern belle" gown. If the veil has lace, be sure it is the same style as the wedding gown. Use bridal magazines as guides; they do a beautiful job of coordinating veils with gowns.

Something Borrowed

No Cost. *$0*

Wear your friend's or relative's headpiece and veil. It has become very popular lately, in fact, for the bride to wear her mother's or grandmother's veil, and it can serve as the "something borrowed" for the bride.

Rent It

Approximate Cost. *$20*

You will find a lovely selection at the rental shops. Again, it is a matter of finding a rental shop convenient to your hometown.

Distress Sale

Approximate Cost. *$20*

Very often the bride who is selling her dress through a classified ad also has her veil for sale. Be sure to ask when you call on the ads because the veil may not be advertised as a separate item. You may, in fact, get the veil thrown in for free with the cost of the dress.

Free Seamstress

Approximate Cost. *$15*

The headpiece and veil are very easy to make. Several seamstresses that I interviewed said that when they make the wedding dress they use leftover netting to assemble a headpiece. The puffed-up, gathered, bouffant-look is popular now, and that is the easiest of all to put together.

Use a ready-made frame, whether it is a full cap, hat or narrow headband. Attach the netting and any other silk flowers, pearls or lace that you wish to add. If you find a headpiece and veil you like in a bridal shop, just buy the necessary embellishments at a fabric store and copy them. Anyone can do this, even someone who doesn't sew. This is what an elegant headpiece and veil would cost to make:

Headband	$ 3.49
Tulle lace, 2 yards, 108″ wide @ $2.98 per yard	5.96
Two silk flowers with pearl edging	2.50
Extra embellishments	3.00
Total	$14.95

Styles of Wedding Veils

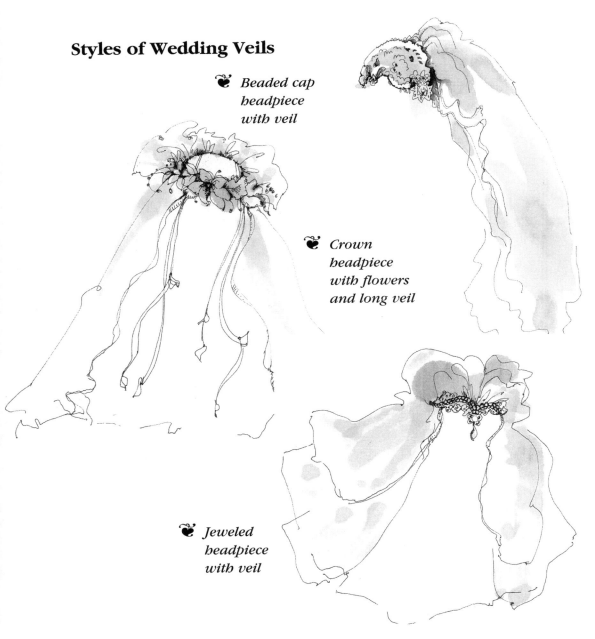

🍂 *Beaded cap headpiece with veil*

🍂 *Crown headpiece with flowers and long veil*

🍂 *Jeweled headpiece with veil*

Bride's veils are based on either a cap or a headband design. Although they look exquisite, they are so simple anyone can make them—even someone who doesn't sew at all. Fabric stores sell a variety of caps and headbands already embellished with pearls, flowers and lace, or you can put together your own creation. Then simply attach the netting and you'll have a stunning veil for a fraction of the retail price.

Hire a Seamstress

Approximate Cost. *$50*

The seamstresses I interviewed charge an average of $50 for the headpiece and veil, including materials and labor. It can run less if it is made from the netting left over from the dress and attached to a very simple cap.

Buy Discount

Approximate Cost. *$75*

Try the factory outlets and catalogs. The JCPenney bridal catalog, for instance, has all their beautiful veils priced at about $75. Your discount Bridal Service representative will also be able to help you. She can find the veil of your choice for 20 to 40 percent off the retail price.

The Bride's Slip

If you decide to purchase a slip in a bridal salon, expect to pay between $75 and $100. This unpleasant added expense can easily be avoided with these ideas:

Something Borrowed

No Cost. *$0*

There are closets all over town cluttered with wedding slips, and you probably know a few of their owners. Drop a few hints here and there and you will find that brides are glad to loan out their wedding petticoats. After our daughter had already purchased hers, she was offered two of them. You may want to wait as long as possible to make this purchase because I am sure one will appear. If nothing lands on your doorstep by three weeks before the wedding, go ahead and use another plan.

Rent It

Approximate Cost. *$10–15*

Most of the slips I saw for rent had lost their "puff." A bouffant nylon slip really doesn't hold its shape for long, so you may want to rent one only if it is fairly new and gives your dress the needed support.

Free Seamstress

Approximate Cost. *$10*

Use white sheeting or muslin fabric for the body of the slip and then add ruffles of stiff nylon netting. The number of ruffles depends upon the fullness of the wedding dress. An average petticoat will require approximately 3⅞ yards of 72-inch netting.

A very full petticoat will require 6 yards. Be sure to make the petticoat as full as necessary in order to give the skirt the support it needs.

If you select a bouffant-skirted formal on the "Prom It" plan, you will definitely need lots of stiff ruffles to achieve the desired look. Sewing your own slip is especially smart in this case since many wedding slips really don't have the necessary fullness. This should be your total cost to sew your own petticoat:

Stiff nylon netting, 6 yards, 72″ @ $1.19 per yard	$ 7.14
Muslin, 2 yards, 45″ @ $.99 per yard	1.98
Thread	.89
Total	$10.01

Hire a Seamstress
Approximate Cost *$30*

A seamstress will charge approximately $20 to make the slip for you. This, added to the cost of the materials, totals $30. Whether you sew it yourself or hire a seamstress, you will have a much sturdier petticoat than you can purchase, with all the fullness needed for your particular wedding gown.

Buy Discount
Approximate Cost *$40*

Look around for sales and bargains at the factory outlet stores. Catalog shopping is also a possibility, and don't forget to check with your Discount Bridal Service representative.

The Bride's Shoes

The bride's shoes can become another unpleasant surprise if you don't shop wisely. As you can imagine, full retail price on her shoes can run over $100 in a bridal or shoe salon. Here are some cost-cutting suggestions:

Something Borrowed
No Cost *$0*

Perhaps you have a friend or relative who will lend you her shoes for the wedding. Remember, they don't have to be "wedding" shoes, only the right shade of white. Be open-minded on this idea, for you may find that someone's dressy white heels might be just what you need. If you are wearing a floor-length gown, the shoe is not as important as you may think. The most important thing is that the shoe is soft and comfortable. Be sure that the heel is not too high and that the shoes are plenty roomy.

They say that your wedding shoe should be one size larger than you normally wear because your feet will swell as the day goes along. You want the shoe to feel like a slipper all day so that you will still feel fresh by the end of the reception.

Buy Discount
Approximate Cost. *$20*

Inexpensive shoes can be found at Payless Shoes, Kmart, Target and other discount stores, as well as factory outlet shops. You don't need a shoe with quality that will last for years; you only need a pair that looks great and feels comfortable for about ten hours. Be sure to shop late in the day when your feet are swollen. Remember that on the day of the wedding your feet will be equally as swollen, or more so, because stress causes additional water retention. Be safe—buy big!

Buy Skimmers
Approximate Cost. *$20*

A bridal "skimmer" is a slipper-type shoe in white satin. It is a very comfortable shoe and comes perfectly flat or with a tiny wedge. I highly recommend this style shoe because of its comfort and low price. It is "wobble-proof" when you walk down the aisle and will guarantee that you will leave on your honeymoon with a "happy back." You may find that a regular ballerina slipper will accomplish this same purpose, and it may cost even less than a skimmer. Both of these slippers are very plain and can be embellished, if you like, with any number of wedding accessories available at your fabric or craft stores. There are white satin rosettes, ribbons, pearls, sequins or lace appliques, all of which can be glued on with "No-Sew" glue or a hot-glue gun.

Our daughter chose plain white satin ballerina flats. Feminine and delicate, they complemented her dress perfectly.

If you are not wearing a floor-length gown, you may want to avoid such a flat shoe, but whatever shoes you choose, be sure to break them in before the wedding. Wear them around the house, covered with a big pair of socks to keep them clean. Stand in them while you do the dishes or iron. Just remember that if you ever wanted a comfortable pair of shoes, it is now.

Now you have ideas for your dress, headpiece, slip and shoes, and at much lower cost than you thought. Don't forget to record all your ideas in the notebook under the "Clothing" section. Which plans sound good to you? Who may be able to loan you a wedding slip? Will Aunt Jenny's veil work? Put your thoughts on paper so that you don't forget them!

Have fun putting it all together—I know you will be a beautiful bride!

4

What a Handsome Bunch!

*(Outfitting the Wedding Party
Without Breaking the Bank)*

Now that the bride is all set, we need to dress the rest of the party. Very few of the expenses described in this chapter are usually borne by the bride's family, except for their personal attire.

The rest of the bridal party, however, including the bridesmaids, junior attendants, groomsmen, flower girl and ring bearer, usually pay their own way. But just in case the bride's family will need to cover any of these expenses, this chapter will offer cost-cutting ideas for each of them.

The Mother's Dress

The mother's dress should blend into the color scheme; it should not clash or stand out as some kind of fashion statement. This is not Mom's high school reunion where she wants to be the slimmest, sexiest woman in the room; this is the bride's day and Mom doesn't want to distract from the bride's gown.

The mother's dress should be somewhat conservative, and not longer or more formal than her daughter's dress. If the bride's dress is tea length or street length, the mother's dress should not be floor length. The mother's dress should be a neutral color or one that complements the bridesmaids' dresses. The style of Mom's dress should also fit in with the wedding's theme. A very contemporary dress, for example, wouldn't be appropriate for a ''Southern Antebellum'' theme.

When I went shopping for my mother-of-the-bride dress, I was appalled at those for sale at the bridal salons. They not only made me feel fat and old, but the prices gave me an upset stomach. Some of the dresses looked like drapes wrapped around with a pin holding them together—and they cost hundreds of dollars! I'll tell you later where I bought my dress, but it definitely was not at a bridal salon.

This is what a mother's dress will cost if purchased at a bridal salon:

AREA	COST
Northeastern States—Metropolitan	$400
Northeastern States	$300
Southeastern States	$300
Midwestern States	$175
Central Mountain States	$225
Northwestern States	$250
Southwestern States	$350
California—Metropolitan	$350
California	$225

Here are ways for Mom to save money:

Something Borrowed
Approximate Cost. $35

If Mom can borrow a dress, her only costs should be alterations, if required.

Rent It
Approximate Cost. $50

You will be delighted with the beautiful dresses available for mother at the rental shops. Some of these dresses would cost as much as $700 to purchase and yet can be rented for as little as $30.

Buy Discount
Approximate Cost. $40

Believe it or not, you can buy a mother's dress at a factory outlet store for as low as $40. Also, try the catalogs and keep your eye on sales everywhere in general.

Free Seamstress
Approximate Cost. $65

The following costs are based on a Simplicity pattern. I walked into my local fabric store and scouted out these materials at regular price. If you shop around for fabric sales, I am sure you could cut the cost considerably.

Pattern	$20.00
Taffeta slip fabric, 1¾ yards, 45″ @ $5.99 per yard	10.48
Chiffon slip flounce, 2½ yards, 45″ @ $4.89 per yard	17.43
Dress fabric, single-edged Galloon lace, 2⅜ yards, 45″ @ $5.98 per yard	14.81
Neck facing, ⅝ yard of 54″ tulle @ $2.98 per yard	1.87
Three ⅜″ buttons @ $.40 each	1.20
Total	$65.79

Hire a Seamstress
Approximate Cost. $115

A seamstress will charge approximately $50 to make a mother-of-the bride dress. This, added onto the cost for the materials, will give you the dress of your choice for about $115.

Buy a "Finer" Dress
Approximate Cost. $150

Go to the Finer Dresses section of your local department store. You'll find styles that are more youthful and becoming, and much less expensive than most mother-of-the-bride dresses. This is where I found my dress on sale for under $50, and I received many compliments on it. The bodice was lined and appliqued with satin flowers that were sprinkled with small pearls. It had a soft, full chiffon skirt and filmy sleeves with satin cuffs. It was cream-colored and compatible with the burgundy color scheme. A soft pink, the wedding's accent color, would also have worked well.

As soon as I found my dress, by the way, I snipped a fabric sample from an inside seam and sent it, along with a photo of the dress, to the mother of the groom who lives in another city. She used this as a guide to purchase her own dress which was very similar to mine in color and style. Both of our dresses were street length.

The Bridesmaids' Dresses

Here is some free advice, worth the price of this book: "DON'T TAKE ALL THE BRIDESMAIDS SHOPPING AT THE SAME TIME!" If all the bridesmaids hop together from place to place, trying on dresses and arguing over styles, you will not only have a wasted day, but you will have a huge headache.

Have you ever been in a restaurant and overheard a group of women arguing over the bill? "No, I had the tuna salad sandwich and coffee. I didn't have a salad at all. Mine should only be $5.75." "Well, I know mine won't be over $6.50 because I had the special," etc. It's embarrassing to watch them with their mini-calculators, haggling away. You are faced with a similar situation when the whole pack of attendants travels en masse, trying on bridesmaids' dresses.

To avoid this entire nightmarish possibility, make a plan ahead of time. Have an idea of the general style of dress you will be looking for, taking into consideration the wedding's theme. Also, have a color family in mind. It is best not to count on an exact color because it will be difficult to find, but you can usually come very close.

Also, consider whether the women can afford to pay retail prices at a bridal salon. Would it be better to have their dresses sewn from a pattern of the bride's choice? Is it unlikely to find a ready-made dress that will be flattering to each of their figures? Also, what about their finances? Even though the attendants traditionally pay for their own clothes, it might be helpful to suggest some cost-cutting ideas. After all, if even one of the bridesmaids is on a tight budget, it would be courteous for all of them to agree to something other than bridal salon prices. As you have probably guessed, I have a number of ways for them to save money.

Meanwhile, if money is no problem (how unlikely!), these are the prices they may expect to pay at a bridal salon:

AREA	COST
Northeastern States—Metropolitan	$185
Northeastern States	$150
Southeastern States	$150
Midwestern States	$110
Central Mountain States	$150
Northwestern States	$150
Southwestern States	$150
California—Metropolitan	$175
California	$150

It is a lot to ask of a working girl to spend this much money to be in her friend's wedding, and these figures don't even include her shoes and slip. Here are some refreshing ways to escape the "bridal salon price trap":

Rent It
Approximate Cost. *$50*

This is the least expensive plan; however, for very little more she can have the "Free Seamstress" plan and end up with a dress she can keep. The bridesmaids' dresses that are available for rent are high quality and, if the shop has them available in the color and sizes you require, this might be the best plan for your friends. Most of the shops will allow alterations.

Free Seamstress
Approximate Cost. *$77*

Under this plan each attendant must arrange for her own volunteer seamstress. The attendants may all go to the fabric store together to purchase the fabric and other materials, or one person may take care of it and be reimbursed later. Here are the materials required for an average Simplicity pattern dress:

Pattern	$15.00
Fabric, 8⅝ yards 45″ taffeta @ $5.99 per yard	51.66
Zipper, 22″	3.00
Thread	1.85
Two ⅜″ buttons for sleeves @ $.40 each	.80
Lace medallion, one	3.50
Interfacing, ½ yard @ $2.29 per yard	1.15
Total	$76.96

You can save quite a bit on the materials by hunting for fabric sales. These are the advantages of using the "Free Seamstress" plan:

- ❧ *You can select the pattern of your choice* that will be flattering to all the attendants' figures.

- ❧ *The dresses will fit perfectly.* When ordering from a bridal salon there is the awful possibility that you discover, at the very last minute, that the dress makes one of the chubbier attendants look like Miss Piggy. When the dresses are sewn at home, the fit can be just right, even if it means making up the bodice first in sheeting fabric. This is a good idea, especially for the extra-bosomy bridesmaid. By making up the bodice in sheeting fabric first, you can see whether the neckline needs to be cut higher. Extremely sexy bridesmaids are not popular with the bride.

- ❧ *You will not have to special order the dresses* through a salon where you cannot be sure that all the dresses will arrive from the manufacturer in time for the wedding. Also, you have the freedom of selecting a color and fabric of your choice. In a salon it may be difficult to find the style you want in the right color and fabric. Usually, there must be a compromise, selecting the dress that comes as close as possible to what the bride really envisioned.

Hire a Seamstress
Approximate Cost. $127

If you have doubts about using a volunteer seamstress, you may want to have the dresses sewn by a professional. The average seamstress's fee for making a bridesmaid's dress is $50. This, added to the price of the materials, will bring the total to approximately $127. Again, most of the seamstresses I spoke with will help shop for the pattern and fabric and will arrive at the wedding ahead of time to make any last-minute alterations. A good seamstress, too, can tell you whether or not a certain style will be suitable for each of the attendants' figures, but she will need to see each woman and take measurements in order to help with this decision.

Buy Discount
Approximate Cost. $40

Try the factory outlets for dresses that can be used in a wedding. In this case, there is no escape from shopping with all the bridesmaids at once. (Bring the aspirin.) If you are lucky, you may find dresses that are alike, one in each size required. It is worth a try, in spite of the hysteria of the day, if the attendants really need to save money. At some of the San Francisco outlets I found fabulous dresses priced as low as $30. Some of the outlets, such as Gunne Sax, have actual bridesmaids' dresses at their bridal location. You may find these dresses for under $50 each.

The next best thing is to try the mail-order catalogs. This is what my daughter did. She selected a dress out of the JCPenney catalog that happened to be perfect in color, fabric and style. The dress was two-piece with a peplum jacket and elegant shirred sleeves. The fabric was a shiny polyester that looked like heavy satin. The color was exactly right—burgundy. She was able to see an actual sample of the fabric at a Penney's bridal salon at a local mall.

Her bridesmaids were scattered: one in Denver, one in San Francisco, one in Fresno and one in our hometown. Each bridesmaid took her own measurements, which determined the size that should be ordered. Then our daughter ordered all of the dresses at one time from the same lot, to be delivered to each girl at her local Penney's store. Each bridesmaid paid for her own dress when she picked it up. It worked great. These dresses were on sale for $60 each and, without the jacket, were quite practical for each girl to wear later, especially when hemmed to street length.

We later saw this *identical* dress, by the way, for sale in a bridal salon for $270!

Bridesmaids' Headpieces

Free Seamstress
Approximate Cost. $2
___

The bridesmaids' headpieces can be made for practically nothing. I made those used for my daughter's wedding at a cost of under $1 each. Luckily, one of the bridesmaids was only about five feet tall and we had a good foot of fabric left over when she had her dress shortened, enough to make four large, flat bows, lined with stiffening from the fabric store. Attached to these bows was gathered burgundy netting that hung to shoulder-length. Where the netting met the bow I added two burgundy silk rosettes and white baby's breath. You do not have to be a seamstress or especially "crafty" to come up with something like this. Just look at the bridesmaids' headpieces for sale in salons or modeled in Bridal magazines and copy them at home.

Flowers and Ribbon
Approximate Cost. $4
___

If you don't want any fuss at all, tie one or two fresh or silk flowers with a piece of satin ribbon that matches the dress. The bridesmaids can wear these on the side or back of their heads.

Hat Plus
Approximate Cost. $10
___

If a hat is the perfect accessory, buy an inexpensive one from a craft store or discount department store; they are often available for under $5. Spray-paint it in the right color and embellish it with all the goodies of your choice—ribbons, rosettes, baby's breath or fabric. Be original—anything goes! (Note: Spray paint works well on cloth and straw hats but don't try it on vinyl or leather, as it will crack.)

Bridesmaids' Slips

Wear Your Own
No Cost. $0
___

Most women have a slip that will work, unless the dress requires one that is quite full, in which case she will need to use another plan.

Something Borrowed
No Cost. $0
___

She can borrow a slip that has been used by either a bride or a bridesmaid.

Rent It

Approximate Cost. **$5–15**

This is a very practical way to go, but it will depend on your proximity to a good rental shop. It may not be worth the drive just to rent a slip.

Free Seamstress

Approximate Cost. **$10**

The materials will cost the same or a little less than for the bride's slip.

Hire a Seamstress

Approximate Cost. **$25**

Again, the cost for materials and labor will be the same or a little less than for the bride.

Bridesmaids' Shoes

Wear Their Own

No Cost. **$0**

Dyed-to-match pumps are no longer expected. It has become quite acceptable for the bridesmaids to wear their own shoes. Of course, all the shoes should be of the same general color, height and style. Women generally have a plain pump that will work with most dresses. If the dress is floor-length, it is really easy to get away with wearing their own shoes. The height of the heel and style of the shoes won't matter; only the color should be the same, and the shoes should be polished and in good repair. Of course, the flatter the shoe, the more comfortable.

Buy Discount

Approximate Cost. **$10–20**

If it is necessary to purchase shoes, go for the most inexpensive you can find. A recent Los Angeles bride found perfect matching pumps for her bridesmaids at Target on sale for $9.99 a pair (this was after finding their dresses at a Lanz outlet in mid-Wilshire at $45 apiece.) Just be sure they are comfortable and a size larger than normal. The bridesmaids don't want pinched toes either.

Buy Skimmers

Approximate Cost. **$20**

Follow the same advice given the bride. A flat, ballerina-style shoe can be the ultimate in comfort. This is especially practical when worn with a floor-length dress.

The Flower Girl's Dress

A dress for a flower girl or junior attendant can cost as much as $125 when purchased at a bridal salon or children's shop. Outfitting these little gals can dig deep into their parents' food budget for the month, and, unfortunately, the rental shops usually do not carry dresses below women's size 6. But don't despair—there are several ways around this dilemma.

Embellish Her Party Dress
Approximate Cost. $5

Most little girls have a special "party dress." It may be a confirmation dress or Easter dress. If you are lucky, like my daughter was, it may be in white or a color that will work in the wedding. My daughter's little niece happened to have a pale pink party dress with a full skirt. She even had her own matching "Mary Jane" shoes. All the dress needed to coordinate with the wedding colors was a big sash, which was easily obtained. Her head was topped with a wreath of flowers, and she looked adorable as she walked down the aisle carrying the basket of flowers.

The sash can be made out of fabric or ribbon of the same color as the bridesmaids' dresses. If you purchase this fabric or ribbon, it will cost about $3; if you have scraps left over from the bridesmaids' dresses, it will be free.

Free Seamstress
Approximate Cost. $42

If the dress can be sewn by a volunteer, here is what you can expect to pay for the materials. These costs are based on a Simplicity pattern:

Pattern	$15.00
Fabric, 3⅛ yards, 45" taffeta @ $5.99 per yard	18.72
Sash, 2 yards, 1½" wide @ $2.00 per yard	4.00
Thread	1.89
Zipper, 12"	2.60
Total	$42.21

One distinct advantage of making the dress is that it can match the bridesmaids' dress, if that is what you want. The pattern books have flower girl and junior attendant patterns that coordinate with wedding dresses and bridesmaids' dresses.

Hire a Seamstress
Approximate Cost. $72

Professional seamstresses charge approximately $30 to make a flower girl's or junior attendant's dress. This, added to the cost of the materials, brings the total to approximately $72. This is still a lot of money, but less than buying retail.

Buy Discount
Approximate Cost. $30

Shop around the discount stores. Look for sales everywhere, too. The JCPenney bridal catalog sells these dresses for about $70, but Penney's *regular* catalog sells suitable dresses for $30 to $35. You should also check out the resale shops that handle children's clothing.

Men's Attire

When a friend or relative of the groom agrees to be a groomsman or usher in the wedding, it is an unspoken understanding that he will pay to rent his own tuxedo. If it will be very difficult for one of the men to handle this expense, it is courteous for the groom to offer to pay for it himself.

Some of the designer tuxedos, such as Pierre Cardin, Christian Dior or Henry Grethel, rent for approximately $125, not including shoes. There are also discount tuxedo rentals available that range from $40 to $50, depending on where you live; these tuxedos are usually copies of the more expensive designer brands. The average costs to rent a tuxedo are given on the next page. These costs include coat, trouser, cummerbund or vest, shirt, bow tie, studs and cufflinks. They sometimes include

AREA	COST
Northeastern States—Metropolitan	$95
Northeastern States	$60
Southeastern States	$60
Midwestern States	$60
Central Mountain States	$60
Northwestern States	$60
Southwestern States	$75
California—Metropolitan	$90
California	$60

alterations and delivery to and from the wedding site. Also, the groom's rental is often free if all the groomsmen rent their tuxedos from the shop. The costs do not include shoes, which rent for $12 to $25 per pair.

The style of the men's tuxedos is determined by the bride's gown. The groom's is usually distinctive from those of the groomsmen. My son-in-law, for example, wore a black tuxedo with tails; his groomsmen wore the same tuxedo, but with a short jacket. The staffs in tuxedo rental shops are helpful in making these decisions and should be consulted as soon as possible. The actual tuxedo rentals can be reserved six months before the wedding, but no later than one month ahead of time.

Often, the men will rent their tuxedo outfits, but wear their own shoes, saving that cost at least. I only have one alternative to renting.

Wear Their Own
No Cost *$0*
_____

An inexpensive way out for the men is to have them all wear dark suits. You will be amazed how uniform they will look, especially when wearing their boutonnieres. If one of the men only has a light suit, find a darker one that he can borrow.

Another alternative, especially if it is an outdoor wedding, is to wear a navy blazer over white trousers; most men already have these hanging in their closets, but if they need to purchase them, they will be practical additions to any man's wardrobe. The father of the bride, by the way, usually wears the same attire as the groomsmen, but the groom's father has the choice of wearing the same attire as the bride's father or wearing a dark suit instead. The bride and groom need to be sensitive to the financial capabilities of the men who have been asked to participate in the wedding. If even one of the men will suffer a financial hardship by renting an outfit, it can be courteous to suggest this alternative.

I do not recommend, however, having the groom wear a tuxedo while his grooms-men wear dark suits. The contrast will be too great. If the men in the party wear their own suits, so must the groom.

Ring Bearer and Boy Attendants

The cost of renting a little tux, plus shoes, bow tie and cummerbund can run close to that of the men's. A little boy looks very cute in a miniature tuxedo, but he can be equally darling for much less money. Here are some ideas:

Wear His Own
Approximate Cost. *$2*
_____

If you are lucky, your little guy will have his own suit. All you will need to provide is a bow tie to coordinate with the wedding colors. It is acceptable, by the way, for the ring bearer to wear his own suit even though the men are wearing tuxedos. If the ring bearer is really young, he can wear a pair of white shorts with a white dress shirt, embellished with a bow tie. When he carries the ring pillow down the aisle, your guests won't notice what he is wearing as much as how he walks and smiles. Luckily, a child doesn't need expensive clothes to be a precious addition to the wedding party.

Buy Discount

Approximate Cost. $35

For less than the cost of renting a tuxedo, the boy's parents can purchase a complete outfit. This way the child will be able to wear the clothes again. Watch for sales at children's shops, shop discount stores and mail-order catalogs, and don't forget to check out resale shops that handle children's clothing!

If the wedding party uses the money-saving ideas in this chapter, they will be relieved of much of what can be a real financial burden. This will also be a great relief to you in planning the wedding; your special day will be extra joyful knowing that no one had to skip a car payment in order to raise the funds.

Your friends and family will perfectly complement you in your gown. I am excited for you, even though I don't know you. What an honor it would be for me to have a picture of your wedding party for my office wall. Remember me if you have any extras!

5
Would a Rose by Any Other Name . . . ?

(Beautiful Flowers on a Budget)

They say you can't fool all of the people all of the time. Not true! You can—especially when it comes to the flowers.

We are going to have so much fun in this chapter. I will give you dozens of ways to fool people. In fact, you will have a hard time keeping a straight face when they rave on, "My, you really splurged on the flowers. You must have spent a fortune." You will humbly thank them, of course, while saying to yourself, "I'll never let them know we only spent $112 on all the flowers combined."

Yes, it *is* possible to spend only $112 on everything, including a sanctuary full of flowers, twenty-five corsages and boutonnieres, the bridal bouquet, five attendants' bouquets, flower girl's basket and all the extra special things you only hoped to afford. I will tell you how. Just remember that you can never have too many flowers and there is certainly no reason to scrimp.

I went to a wedding once where money was a real problem and they did scrimp. Unfortunately, it really showed. There were no flowers in the church at all and each bridesmaid carried a single daisy. The bride had a nice little bouquet and the groom had a rose in his lapel, but the rest of the men wore no boutonnieres at all. They had obviously decided that the flowers were a good place to cut costs, but they didn't realize the importance of flowers at a wedding. A wedding without flowers feels like a day in traffic court—there just isn't a festive atmosphere.

Flowers have traditionally been an important part of the wedding ceremony. They denote celebration and congratulation; they fill the room with joy! You must have flowers, and as many as you can afford. And you will find that you can afford a lot more than you thought after reading this chapter.

First of all, you need to know what professional florists charge for an average-priced wedding—their prices vary by geographic area. For example, The Tulip Tree in Nashville charges $100 to $250 for the bride's bouquet, $50 and up for each bridesmaid's

bouquet and $5 and up for each boutonniere, whereas at Glass and Green Florists in Livonia, New York, the total bill may only be between $300 and $400. Average floral package prices nationwide usually include:

- ❦ One bridal bouquet in colonial, arm bouquet or cascade design

- ❦ Attendants' bouquets in a colonial style or arm bouquet for one maid of honor and three bridesmaids

- ❦ Two mothers' corsages

- ❦ Four grandmothers' corsages

- ❦ Twelve boutonnieres

- ❦ Two altar arrangements

- ❦ Flower girl basket

AREA	AVERAGE COST
Northeastern States—Metropolitan	$1050
Northeastern States	$ 575
Southeastern States	$ 600
Midwestern States	$ 625
Central Mountain States	$ 425
Northwestern States	$ 700
Southwestern States	$ 725
California—Metropolitan	$ 950
California	$ 550

These prices are shocking, aren't they? And they don't include reception flowers or any of the extras, such as corsages for your guest book attendants. But before you sink into a depression, let me tell you about six money-saving alternatives. They will get you excited—I guarantee!

The first plan will save you the most money, but even if it isn't feasible to "borrow" all the flowers, you may be able to cut costs by getting at least some of them donated.

Free Florist
Approximate Cost. $112

All the flowers and greenery you can use are waiting to be donated or loaned. There are people out there who can hardly wait to provide you with everything you need—for free!

Private gardens are full of flowers, shrubs, evergreens, ferns and flowering bushes. And the best news is that these gardens belong to your friends, relatives and local garden club members who are notoriously generous people. Their lovely flowers are just waiting for your approval. In fact, people with green thumbs are some of the nicest I know and they feel honored that anyone wants to show off their flowers in a wedding.

If you are brave, you might even knock on neighbors' doors if you see something in their yards that would be helpful. You may find that they not only offer you cut flowers but will gladly haul out their ladders and pruning shears to cut down branches of their blooming dogwood trees. Of course, for a good part of the country in the dead of winter there will only be a few things available, such as evergreen boughs or pyracantha berries. But people will often offer baskets, vases, indoor plants, trellises and anything else you see as well.

It may surprise you that people get so mushy over weddings, but even the hardest heart seems to soften at the thought of the loving couple. It also doesn't hurt to look as pitiful as possible when you ask for help!

Another ingenious source of free flowers is to plant them yourself in your own garden, to be "harvested" a day or so before the wedding. This way you will have the exact type and quantity of flower you need.

Your local nursery is another wonderful source of free plants, shrubs and trees. They will sometimes loan a certain number of their plants at no charge. We borrowed fifteen huge potted evergreen trees for our daughter's reception that turned the hall into a winter wonderland.

If your wedding is planned for the spring or summer, keep your eyes open for fields of wildflowers; these flowers add an interesting and delicate touch to the corsages. They can also be used to make up massive arrangements for the reception. Watch for delights such as Queen Anne's Lace, black-eyed Susans, daisies, asters and goldenrod. Be sure to shake out any little critters who may have made these flowers their home.

The church or synagogue itself can also be a source of free flowers, particularly if the wedding is planned for a time when it is already decorated for another reason. For example, our daughter's wedding was in December when the church had a twenty-five-foot tree covered with tiny white lights, railings draped with garlands of flowers and pillars dripping with ribboned evergreen sprays.

These are some of the flowers normally used for weddings: roses, spider mums, carnations, orchids, lilacs, daisies, asters, bells of Ireland, lilies, stephanotis and baby's breath. But be open-minded to anything you see that is growing. You don't have to use traditional flowers; be creative—try something unusual. You may be interested to know that there are florists who win awards for their wedding arrangements because of their creative uses of nontraditional flowers. These florists are even employed by the "rich and famous" to come up with something different. People are trying to get away from the same old thing. So, look upon free flowers with great glee, and if they don't win you an award, just let me know and I'll send you one!

I am assuming you will be able to borrow all the baskets and vases you will need, so your only cost will be the supplies listed below. These can be purchased from a floral supply store.

SUPPLIES	COST
Acetate ribbon, 100 yards, 1½″ wide	$ 9.35
Acetate ribbon, 100 yards, 3″ wide	9.10
Acetate ribbon, 100 yards, ⅝″ wide	5.50
Satin ribbon for streamers, 8 yards	3.84
Florist wire, three boxes	11.00
Florist tape, 60 yards	2.80
Plastic bouquet holder, six	19.50
Ready-made corsage forms, four	10.00
Corsage pins, two packages	1.00
Net, ½ yard, 6″ wide	2.00
Stemmed corsage inserts (pearls, rosettes, etc.)	3.00
Tablecloth lace, ½ yard	3.50
Other corsage embellishments (satin leaves, etc.)	5.00
Baby's breath, two sprays	10.00
Stardust Gypsy, two sprays	5.50
Forty small silk flowers such as lilies of the valley, stephanotis, bells of Ireland, etc.	11.37
Total	$112.46

When you are at the floral supply store, ask for a free demonstration in making corsages, bouquets and bows. This is what I did and was surprised at how easy it is to learn. They even have bouquets and corsages made up for you to see as examples.

Later you can use brides' magazines and florists' brochures for ideas. But don't forget the importance of being original, too.

The folks at the floral supply will show you the easy way to make the bride's and attendants' bouquets by using a plastic bouquet holder as a base. It has a handle that fastens to a doilied cup with hidden oasis, the damp block that holds the flowers firmly in place while keeping them watered. Just insert the flower stems into the oasis, along with some trailing ribbons or some ivy. It is so simple.

The same is true for the corsages. You will learn to use the wire and tape to hold the flowers in place. It is so much fun you may be tempted to open your own flower shop. You will only need to use the ready-made forms for the larger corsages; the rest will be fine with ribbon, greenery and other embellishments added; they should be made up the day before the wedding and refrigerated.

The last seven items on the supply list can be used to give the bouquets and corsages that professional look. The tablecloth lace is to be cut up into lace strips, saving the cost of buying lace by the yard. Cut the lace into whatever widths you need. Make full loops of lace two or three inches wide for the bouquets, or very narrow strips to place on top of the ribbon in the corsages.

The narrow satin ribbon should be used only for the streamers in the bouquets and flower girl basket. Tie several knots in these streamers; it helps them hang nicely. Acetate ribbon will not work because it won't tie into these pretty love knots.

The men's boutonnieres are the simplest of all to make. Use a single flower, usually a tight rosebud, and wrap the stem with florist's tape, working in something delicate and white, such as baby's breath. You don't even need a ribbon for these, so they make up very quickly.

You can't go wrong on the flower girl's basket—just be sure it isn't too large and has a handle. Fill it with flowers and trail some of the satin ribbon. Wire a few of the same flowers together to make a wreath or hairpiece; add some ribbon and baby's breath, and she will look adorable.

After you have assembled and refrigerated the bouquets, boutonnieres and the flower girl's basket, start decorating the church and reception hall. You will need to transport boxes full of flowers, greenery and supplies, including scissors, tape, etc. When you arrive at the church to do your decorating, you will feel confident because you will have so much to work with. That is the way it is with the ''free florist''—you don't have to scrimp. Just be sure to have plenty of volunteers so you won't feel pressured.

With the clergyman's permission, attach flowers, greenery and ribbon to the pews, windows, pillars, candelabra, altar tables and the tops of the organ and piano. Use a little watered oasis to keep everything fresh throughout the wedding, except for the evergreen boughs which are hardy and need no help. Make garlands for doorways and staircases by wiring greenery and ribbon together. You would need a bank loan to pay a professional florist for all these extras.

The same is true in the reception hall. You will have plenty of flowers and greenery to decorate walls, doorways, arches, trellises, tables, the cake, punch bowl and cake knife. Since cost is not a factor, you can go wild.

Styles of Bouquets

🌿 *Arm Bouquet*

🌿 *Cascade*

Colonial and cascade-style bouquets use a holder with oasis as a base; the arm bouquet is simply a bunch of flowers tied with ribbon to be carried on your arm.

If you run out of a certain color flower while you are decorating the church and hall, do what florists do—spray paint some tufts of greenery to fill in. I suggest that you have a small can of paint on hand just in case this happens; buy it in your primary wedding color.

You will find many advantages to the "free florist" plan. The main advantage, of course, is that it is the least expensive way to go. Another is the great sense of satisfaction in the creativity. Every corsage will be special and unique. The baskets of flowers will be unlike any your guests have ever seen. After all, the same florists have probably been doing the weddings in your town for years—it is definitely time for some originality.

Obviously, one of the greatest advantages is that you will be able to have more flowers and larger arrangements than you could have afforded otherwise. How else can you provide all those extra corsages, the garlands along the bannisters and the pew flowers? There is no doubt you will need to supply smelling salts for those guests who swoon at your opulence!

One of the nicest things about this plan, too, is the fun your volunteers will have putting it all together. It can be a real party in itself. You may have had doubts about their artistic capabilities, but you will be surprised how easily it all goes together. There is something exhilarating about converting piles of flowers and supplies into beautiful works of art. Be sure that you have used your notebook to keep track of these volunteers, as well as those who provided flowers. You'll want to thank them for their kindness.

There are a couple of disadvantages to the plan, however. If you live in a big city, there aren't as many gardens. You will need to arrange with your country friends and relatives to bring their cuttings to you a few days before the wedding. Just be sure to cut the stems *under water* so they will keep until you will be using them. This prevents air pockets from forming and will force intake of water into the stalks. They will stay fresh for several days this way.

This plan also has a distinct disadvantage to the bride who will be having a winter wedding in a northern state. It will be difficult to find anything blooming at that time of year. One solution is the old spray-paint trick—"make" flowers out of certain shrubs and greenery. Otherwise, the winter bride may want to use silk flowers as explained in the next money-saving plan.

Fool Them with Silks
Approximate Cost. $224

This plan is similar to the "Free Florist" plan except that you will use silk flowers in place of fresh. You will still need some filler foliage from your yard or florist and the same supplies from the floral supply store.

There are hundreds of silk flowers to choose from. They will average $.50 per flower when purchased from an Oriental import outlet, such as Cost Plus or Pier 1 Imports. The beautifully realistic flowers are made by hand in Korea and China. Just be picky and select only those flowers that look exactly like the real thing. Here is a sampling

How to Make a Garland

Cut your greenery to a uniform length—eight to twelve inches is good. Bunch several lengths of greenery in your hand, then wrap them with florist wire, leaving some wire hanging. Add another clump of greens so that it overlaps the first, and reinforce it with wire. Continue adding bunches and wrapping with florist wire until the garland reaches the desired length.

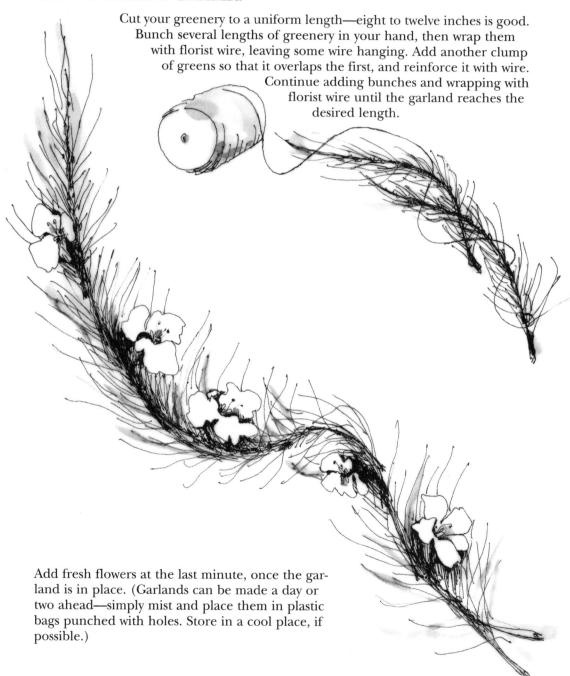

Add fresh flowers at the last minute, once the garland is in place. (Garlands can be made a day or two ahead—simply mist and place them in plastic bags punched with holes. Store in a cool place, if possible.)

of silk flower prices with the column price indicating how much *each* individual flower costs. By the way, whenever you can, *always* buy a spray of flowers instead of single stems. A spray has a number of flowers on small stems that shoot off a main stem.

Rose, hand-wrapped (eight roses per spray)	$ .87
Carnations, miniature (six carnations per spray)	.33
Carnations, large (twelve carnations per spray)	.55
Gypsophila, six sprigs	.65
Orchids, the highest quality and most realistic	4.00
Daisies, medium (twenty per bush)	.18
Gardenias, highest quality and most realistic	2.00
Larkspur, tall	.40

Your costs may be slightly more or less, depending on the flowers you select and how close you live to a large import outlet. Here is one case where big-city brides have an advantage—the larger the city, the better your prices on silk flowers and floral supplies is likely to be.

If you don't live near a big city, it will be worth the trip for the money you will save, as well as the selection. The residents of the little town where I live shop the discount market in San Francisco all the time. It is two hours away, but worth the drive.

Now that you have an idea of the prices, here is an actual budget for a wedding done in silk flowers. I have listed everything you will need.

Bride's bouquet, twenty flowers @ $.68 ea.	$ 13.60
Attendants' bouquets, fifteen flowers @ $.68 ea.	10.20
Flower girl's basket, fifteen flowers @ $.68 ea.	10.20
Boutonnieres, fifteen single roses @ $.40 ea.	6.00
Two mothers' corsages, orchids, @ $4 ea.	8.00
Four grandmothers' corsages, five flowers ea. (roses or miniature carnations) @ $.57 ea.	11.40
Ten other corsages, two carnations per corsage @ $.50 ea. or one gardenia @ $1 ea.	10.00

Two baskets of tall altar flowers, such as lark-spur, forty-eight flowers @ $.40 ea.		19.20
Pew flowers, two per pew × twenty pews @ $.36 ea.		14.40
One low table arrangement of miniature carnations for reception, thirty flowers @ $.30 ea.		9.00
	Subtotal	$112.00
Plus supplies, as listed in the ''Free Florist'' plan		$112.00
	Total	$224.00

Once you have purchased the silk flowers and supplies, put them together following the same procedures described in the ''Free Florist'' plan, but first, rip the flowers from the stems and glue them to the stems or branches, so they're secure. This is especially important with boutonnieres—you don't want the single flower to fall off leaving just a stem.

There are two terrific advantages to this silk flower plan. One is that you can make up the flowers ahead of time. This means you won't have to worry that Aunt Minnie got lost driving to your house with her prize roses or that someone's camellias got pelted by a hailstorm. Another plus is that you won't be as rushed the day before the wedding.

The main disadvantage is that you will not have fresh flowers at the wedding. Some people actually prefer silk flowers, but, if this is a problem for you, why not order a few things from the florist? A nice choice would be the bride's bouquet and the mothers' corsages. This will add a little expense, but you will still be saving a great deal of money by doing the rest of the wedding in silks.

Fool Them with the Real Thing
Approximate Cost. $300–350

With this plan you will need to purchase fresh flowers from a wholesale flower mart. The costs vary only slightly throughout the United States and here, again, the big-city bride has the advantage because the best wholesale markets are in the large cities. You can find them by looking under ''Florists'' in your Business-to-Business Yellow Pages.

In some parts of the country, wholesale flower marts may not be open to the public. If this is the case in your town, look for a florist who will work with you to keep costs down. For instance, some florists will sell you bunches of flowers at substantially reduced rates if you do the arranging yourself. (In effect, the retail florist acts as a wholesaler, eliminating the service expense.) Also, if you know what kinds of flowers and colors you want but are willing to remain flexible, a florist may be able to give you a special deal at the last minute—just wait to see what's on sale the week of the wedding. By the way, if your wedding is in the spring, you may be able to purchase armloads of peach, apple, almond or cherry blossoms directly from orchard owners at a very low cost.

Enough fresh flowers for an average wedding will cost between $200 and $250. You will also need the same supplies mentioned in the first two plans. This will bring your total cost to between $300 and $350.

The main advantage of this plan is that you will have fresh flowers. One disadvantage is that you will have to transport the flowers from your nearest wholesale mart at the last minute. Another disadvantage is that you and your volunteers must make them up the day before the wedding, using the same procedure as the ''Free Florist'' plan.

Supermarket Wedding Package
Approximate Cost. *$250*

The supermarket chains not only bake wedding cakes in their bakeries and prepare reception food in their deli departments, but also offer lovely, affordable floral packages. Call several in your own hometown to compare plans, but to give you an idea of what you can get for the money, here are two wedding packages offered recently by the Lucky Stores chain:

''Bride's Delight'' *$169.99*

Includes:

- ❦ One bridal bouquet, cascade style (9 roses, 12 mini-carnations)

- ❦ One bridesmaid's bouquet, round style (8 pom-poms, 12 mini-carnations, 3 roses)

- ❦ One groom's boutonniere (a single rose)

- ❦ One best man's boutonniere (a single carnation)

- ❦ Two mother's corsages (mini-carnations)

- ❦ Two father's boutonnieres (a single carnation)

- ❦ One altar or table arrangement

- ❦ One free bridal ''toss bouquet''

"Memories" $229.00

Includes:

- ❦ One bridal bouquet, cascade style (12 roses, 10 mini-carnations, plus pom-poms)

- ❦ Two bridesmaid's bouquets, round style (5 roses, 6 mini-carnations, plus pom-poms)

- ❦ One groom's boutonniere (2 roses)

- ❦ One best man's boutonniere (a single rose)

- ❦ One usher's boutonniere (a single rose)

- ❦ Four corsages (2 roses, 3 mini-carnations)

- ❦ Four boutonnieres (single carnation)

- ❦ One altar or table arrangement

- ❦ One free bridal "toss bouquet"

Share the Joy

Sharing the joy means that two brides go together to share the cost of the professional florist's wedding package. It seems that this would save each bride a great deal of money, but remember that only the church and reception flowers can be shared. It would be a little tacky to take back corsages and boutonnieres that have been given as gifts. And since only one-third of the cost is for the church and reception flowers, that is the amount that would be split between two brides. In order to find another bride, you will need to ask around or watch the engagement announcements in your local newspaper.

This means that each bride would save approximately one-half of the one-third, or 17 percent of the total cost. Therefore, the chart on the next page would be each bride's floral expense.

The advantage here, of course, is the money savings. A disadvantage is that someone may have to transport the flowers from one site to another; there would also need to be a compatible color scheme.

Timing is everything in this scenario. There needs to be plenty of time to transport the flowers from the first site to the second site. Of course, if both weddings are at the same site, this simplifies things. Sharing wedding flowers usually works best when there is one sanctuary decorated in white (or a neutral color) that can be used for two weddings in one day, one in the morning and the other in the late afternoon or evening.

AREA	AVERAGE COST
Northeastern States—Metropolitan	$740
Northeastern States	$475
Southeastern States	$496
Midwestern States	$538
Central Mountain States	$322
Northwestern States	$558
Southwestern States	$588
California—Metropolitan	$683
California	$392

Rent the Showpieces

Here is an interesting idea: Whether you use silk flowers or wholesale flowers, rent the main floral arrangements for the church and reception. The rental prices vary, but an average seems to be in this range:

Two large baskets of gladioli and mums—$45/pair

You will also find the bride's and attendants' bouquets for rent, but the ones I looked at seemed very "used." The large arrangements are in better condition and worthy of consideration; rental stores carry various types of arrangements from roses to dogwood. The most common, however, seem to be baskets of glads and mums.

You may also want to consider renting six-foot pew candlesticks which will add an extremely elegant and dramatic look to the sanctuary. Decorate these tall candlesticks with ribbon, tulle netting or trailing silk, live ivy and any silk or live flowers of your choice.

The Combination Plan

With this plan, you order some of the flowers from a florist; the rest you assemble yourself. Order only the following:

- ❧ Bride's bouquet
- ❧ Attendants' bouquets
- ❧ Boutonnieres
- ❧ Flower girl's basket
- ❧ Corsages

All the church and reception flowers will be on the ''Free Florist'' plan. The only supplies you will need are the large ribbon and some wire, so you will still be saving about one third off the professional florist's average price.

This ''Combination Plan'' is what worked best for our daughter's wedding. We used the church's decorations, free trees at the reception and pine boughs where we could. No one needed smelling salts, but we did receive many compliments. Our total cost was $289. The advantages of this plan are the cost savings and the small amount of work at the last minute.

AREA	**TOTAL COST**
Northeastern–Metropolitan	$598
Northeastern States	$382
Southeastern States	$398
Midwestern States	$432
Central Mountain States	$258
Northwestern States	$449
Southwestern States	$465
California—Metropolitan	$549
California	$315

Floral Advice

I hope one of these plans will work for you and help save you money. And are you remembering your notebook? You should be making note of the plans that appeal to you and any sources of flowers, offers from volunteers, or prices that you may accumulate along the way. Meanwhile, whatever way you go, here are a few tidbits of advice:

- If the bride is tall, she should carry a cascading bouquet; if she is short, she needs a smaller one.

- The bride can carry a Bible or prayer book in place of a bouquet. Just place a flower on top with some white satin ribbon streamers.

- Attendants' bouquets should be smaller and more colorful than the bride's and the maid or matron of honor's bouquet should be a little larger than the other attendants'.

❦ If a church has a high ceiling, use tall altar flowers, if the church has a low ceiling, use a low arrangement.

❦ If a wedding is at night, use white flowers. Dark colors get lost in the shadows and soft lighting.

❦ Both mothers' corsages should be the same to avoid any hard feelings.

❦ If you use the "Free Florist" plan, pick the flowers slighty closed so they won't be too full on the wedding day; be especially careful to select "tight" rosebuds.

❦ If you find some used silk flowers that need a lift, just shake them in a bag with salt. They will look like new.

❦ If you do order from a florist, be sure to order "in-season" flowers. "Out-of-season" flowers are very expensive.

❦ When you have chosen the floral plan that best suits your budget, be sure to outline it in your notebook. Then record each expense.

Note: You may want to consider these cost-cutting alternatives to the traditional bouquet for the bride or her attendants.

❦ *Hand-Tied Nosegay*
Six to eight blooms with only six inches of stalk, tied simply with two trailing ribbons.

❦ *Hand-Tied Arm Bouquet*
This is one of the easiest and more affordable ideas of all: take a spray of fresh flowers, tie the stems with a single wide ribbon.

❦ *Tussie-Mussie Bouquet*
This dainty option works well for a country or Victorian wedding: hand-tie a cluster of dried flowers with ribbons and insert them into a silver, cone-shaped tussie mussie (available at your floral supply store).

❦ *A White Fan Decorated With Flowers*
Purchase a ready-made lace, paper or bamboo fan that can be covered with white satin and lace and then embellished with a single flower, such as an orchid. Or, trail narrow satin ribbons or glue white pearl beads randomly over the satin and lace.

❦ *Round or Heart-Shaped Wreath*

Decorate Styrofoam or grapevine wreaths with lace, bows and trailing ribbons. Add a 10-inch loop of fabric or ribbon at the top of the wreath to be slipped over the wrist.

❦ *Decorated Candy Cane*

If you're having a Christmas wedding, decorate a giant candy cane with holly, mistletoe, sprigs of evergreens, silk stephanotis, white gypsophila, plus ribbon sprinkled with "gold dust" or "white snow" sparkles.

❦ *White Fur Muff*

For any winter wedding, but especially one with a Christmas theme, create fur muffs from white rabbit fur or fake fur fabric; decorate them with a miniature nosegay or a single flower, plus narrow trailing ribbons.

❦ *Sheaves of Wheat*

Borrow from the pure simplicity of an early Roman wedding and carry a sheaf of wheat tied with a single fabric ribbon. This idea works beautifully with a Greco-Roman or Medieval theme, especially when the bridal attendants wear authentic costumes. It also works with an informal, simple outdoor wedding where the bride's and her attendants' dresses are sewn from natural fabrics, such as cotton or wool.

Isn't saving money fun? I know it is exciting for you to plan the flowers for your own special wedding, and I hope my research has helped you out. Let me know if anyone swoons.

6

What's Cookin'?

(Fabulous Food for Pennies per Person)

I know that your niece's reception at the Hotel Ritz cost $8,000 and your friend's catered garden reception cost $5,500, but I have done your research and there are wonderful ways to throw a great party for a fraction of those outrageous costs. Nationwide, wedding receptions average about $7,500.

First of all, have you set the time of the wedding? According to our calendar, one of the first duties is to set the date and location of the wedding. But if you haven't selected the time of day as yet, you may want to give this some thought: the time of the wedding can dictate the cost of the reception food. Here are some guidelines:

Morning wedding ....Continental breakfast or
(before 11 A.M.)   breakfast buffet

Midday wedding ....Luncheon buffet
(11 A.M. to 1 P.M.)

Afternoon wedding ....Hors d'oeuvres buffet or
(1 to 4 P.M.)   Cake and punch only

Early evening wedding ......Dinner buffet
(4 to 7 P.M.)

Evening wedding ....Hors d'oeuvres buffet or
(after 7 P.M.)   Cake and punch only

Obviously, an afternoon or evening wedding will require the least food. But before I tell you about the exciting cost-cutting plans for receptions at any hour, here are the average costs for a professional, fully catered reception in two categories: Hors d'Oeuvres Buffet and Cold Luncheon Buffet. The prices were given to me by catering services all over the country and include the following:

Hors d'Oeuvres Buffet

Miniature meatballs on frill picks

Egg rolls

Vegetable trays with dip

Fresh fruit on frill picks

Coffee, tea and punch

Cold Luncheon Buffet

Trays of sliced roast beef, ham, turkey and Swiss and American cheese

Relish tray of tomatoes, olives and pickle spears

Assorted rolls

Pasta salad

Carrot and raisin salad

Fresh fruit compote

Cucumber salad

Coffee, tea and punch

AREA	HORS D'OEUVRES	COLD LUNCHEON
Northeastern—Metropolitan	$9.50/person	$11.95/person
Northeastern States	$7.95/person	$10.75/person
Southeastern States	$7.60/person	$10.25/person
Midwestern States	$7.35/person	$ 9.95/person
Central Mountain States	$7.75/person	$10.25/person
Northwestern States	$7.80/person	$10.85/person
Southwestern States	$8.30/person	$11.20/person
California—Metropolitan	$8.75/person	$11.60/person
California	$7.60/person	$10.20/person

I selected these particular types of reception foods because they are two of the least expensive available professionally. The costs go much higher, as you can imagine. Sit-down dinners run from $15 to $80 per person, plus about $18 per hour for each waiter or waitress. There is also a ''service fee'' that may or may not include dishes and utensils, setup, cleanup, table linens, table decorations or personal bartender. An open bar, by the way, will cost you approximately $6 per person for each hour of the reception and champagne added to the punch will cost an extra $4 per person.

In order to use my ideas for economy receptions, you must keep one thing in mind: Your reception site must allow you control over the food and beverage that will be served. If you hastily reserve your local club, restaurant or a hotel for your reception, you will be disappointed later to find that you *must* order the reception food and beverage from their caterer, and the per person prices may shock you! To avoid this scenario, rent a reception site through your city, county or state government offices or your local historical society. These sites often rent for under $200, which will save you a bundle in itself, but they will also allow you to bring in your own food and beverage. Because the reception food is the biggest cost of any wedding, this is an important factor. You can literally save thousands of dollars by selecting the right site. And these sites are nothing to be ashamed of—you may find a lovely rose garden, lakeside park or beautifully decorated senior center. Another idea is to reserve the indoor or outdoor reception areas connected to your church or synagogue. These sites are often available for under $100, the cost of janitorial cleanup. (See chapter ten for more site possibilities.)

Once you have safely reserved a site that gives you control, you will be ready for my economy plans. They include foods that are inexpensive and easy to prepare, even by the most mediocre cook. For all you fabulous cooks out there who like to play Julia Child on weekends, you will find that these uncomplicated menus will be a welcome relief, especially as the day approaches. All the food is attractive and delicious and guaranteed to make your guests happy. If the guests are rude enough to ask where the food came from, just say, "Oh, it was prepared by many loving hands." They don't need to know whose.

The starred items on the following menu plans are foods that can be prepared and frozen ahead of time. Be sure to prepare and freeze ahead any foods that you can, up to six months in advance of the wedding. Keep track of these preparations in your notebook. They will undoubtedly be stored in the freezers of friends and relatives all over town, so you will need to keep a nice, neat list of what is where. The more you can accomplish in the weeks before the wedding, the more effortless it will seem on the big day.

By the way, whenever I mention "wholesale food suppliers," I am referring to those food stores that not only sell to restaurants and catering services, but the general public as well. The food is of superior quality and prices are a fraction of those at your local supermarket. Many of my friends, in fact, purchase all their family foods from a wholesaler. You find the same name brands you are used to, but in bulk. All the prices are in addition to the wedding cake, which is covered later in this chapter.

Cost-Cutting Plans for the Reception Food

The Family Plan
Cost . . . . *$.35/person, $105/300 guests*

Family members not only prepare all the food for the reception, but pay for it as well. This is the way wedding receptions were usually handled in the "olden days," but, unfortunately, this old-fashioned generosity is not seen as frequently in the 1990s.

When it is seen, it is usually in a very close family where it has become a tradition to help give the reception for each bride as she comes along.

The family members decide, with the help of the bride and her family, who should bring what type of food, keeping the wedding theme in mind. If the reception has a Hawaiian luau decor, for example, the family may decide upon hollowed-out pineapples filled with fruit, Hawaiian breads, barbecued pork and roasted potato skins. There will usually be at least one talented aunt or grandma with the "gift of hospitality" who can come up with the menu. The family members prepare and store the food in their own homes until the day of the wedding.

Other than approving the menu, the bride and her family are relieved of any responsibilities other than the slight cost per person to cover the paper products, if required, such as plates, utensils, napkins, cups and plastic tumblers.

Cake and Beverage Only
Cost . . . . **$1.21/person, $363/300 guests**

Paper products	$ .35
Coffee, tea and champagne punch	.70
Mints	.06
Nuts	.10
Total	$1.21/person

(The cake, of course, is an additional cost.)

The Pro-Am Combo
Cost . . . . **$1.98/person, $594/300 guests**

Under this plan the main meat dishes are purchased from a professional source, such as a delicatessen, caterer or food service supplier. All the side dishes, such as salads, breads, condiments, vegetable trays, fruit trays or chips and dips, are donated by family and friends. When friends or relatives ask if there is anything they can do to help, have a list of ideas with you in your notebook at all times, and suggest a couple of side dishes for the reception. People really are happy to help if you are ready with suggestions.

*Lasagne	$ .75
*Meatballs	.28
Paper products	.35
Coffee, punch and champagne punch	.60
Total	$1.98/person

*Can be made and frozen ahead of time.

I found delicious lasagne and meatballs for sale at Smart and Final, a wholesale food supplier, for example. The lasagne came in trays of sixteen servings for $11.00 and the meatballs were frozen in a huge plastic sack, 190 medium meatballs for about $15.00. I figured one serving of lasagne and three meatballs per person.

Amateur Hors d'Oeuvres
Cost . . . . $2.59/person, $777/300 guests

*Meatballs on frill picks	$ .32
Fruit kabobs on mini-skewers	.33
*Frozen pizza squares	.32
*Egg rolls	.29
Olives	.10
Pickles	.12
Mints	.06
Nuts	.10
Paper products	.35
Coffee, tea and champagne punch	.60
Total	$2.59/person

*Can be made and frozen ahead of time.

The meatballs, fruit, pizza squares and egg rolls can be purchased from a wholesale food supplier. The fruit kabobs are made by sticking wooden skewers through fresh or frozen fruit pieces. They are then poked into a head of red cabbage which creates a colorful table display. Just be sure to flatten the bottom of the cabbage so it won't roll around.

The reason this breakfast menu is so reasonable is that the meat cost is kept to a minimum by merely sprinkling ham pieces into the eggs. The biscuits and the cinnamon rolls can be purchased from the wholesale food service suppliers. The Potatoes O'Brien come frozen in your supermarket. The apples need to be cored, sprinkled with cinnamon and sugar and baked upright for one hour at 325 degrees—delicious! Most reception kitchens will have ovens to accommodate this number of apples; otherwise, they will need to be done, twenty-five at a time, in the home ovens of friends and family members. It isn't necessary for the apples to be served hot out of the oven; just so they aren't served cold.

The orange juice can be made from concentrate or poured straight from the can. Just float a few orange slices and add a little champagne for sparkle!

This buffet is very tricky because the eggs and potatoes need to be prepared and served hot at the last minute. You will need at least two volunteers to keep three skillets of scrambled eggs going all the time. Whip the eggs ahead of time so that the cooks have nothing to do but "scramble." This breakfast buffet is guaranteed to please your guests without wiping out your life savings.

Amateur Breakfast Buffet
Cost . . . . $2.52/person, $756/300 guests

Scrambled eggs with ham bits	$ .27
*Biscuits	.30
*Cinnamon rolls	.36
*Potatoes O'Brien	.43
Baked apples	.21
Coffee, tea and orange juice/champagne punch	.60
Paper products	.35
Total	$2.52/person

*Can be made and frozen ahead of time.

Amateur Luncheon Buffet
Cost . . . . $3.13/person, $939/300 guests

Dolly roll sandwiches	$ .51
Fruit salad	.33
Potato salad	.30
Mixed bean salad	.33
Pickled beet salad	.33
Olives	.10
Pickles	.12
Nuts	.10
Mints	.06
Coffee, tea and champagne punch	.60
Paper products	.35
Total	$3.13/person

The fruit salad is sold by wholesale suppliers by the gallon. It can be poured into bowls for serving. The potato salad comes in ten-pound cartons. The mixed bean salad and pickled beets come in a can already prepared. The Dolly sandwiches will get rave reviews and are so easy to prepare that I am almost embarrassed to give you this recipe.

For each 100 guests

One twenty-pound turkey

One gallon jar of mayonnaise

Chopped celery (one hundred short pieces, ready to chop, or approximately five pounds)

Salt and pepper to taste

Dolly rolls

The mayonnaise and celery chunks can be purchased from the wholesale supplier. The mayonnaise costs $4.15 per gallon and the celery is $4. The Dolly rolls are available from a bakery at approximately $.15 each when purchased twenty-four at a time. They are the size of a tennis ball and make a filling and delectable sandwich. I have allowed two of these sandwiches per guest.

Bake the turkey in your oven, unstuffed, per directions. Strip all the meat off the turkey, both light and dark, and put it through a meat grinder. Add the mayo and chopped celery. The turkey can be baked, stripped and frozen months in advance. The mayo and celery can be added a day or two before the reception and refrigerated in large resealable bags. Then, during the reception itself, one or two volunteers place "puffy scoops" inside the Dolly rolls and serve the sandwiches fresh on buffet platters. By using a small ice cream scoop, the actual preparation goes very fast. In order to prevent spoilage, it is important to keep the turkey-mayo mixture cold until it's scooped onto the buns.

Amateur Dinner Buffet
Cost . . . . *$3.55/person, $1,065/300 guests*

*Baked half-breasts of chicken	$ .95
*Parsley potatoes	.27
*Glazed whole red beets	.21
Fruit salad compote cups	.40
*Rolls	.12
Tomato slices	.15
*Butter chips	.12
Olives	.10
Pickles	.12
Nuts	.10

Mints	.06
Coffee, tea and champagne punch	.60
Paper products	.35
Total	$3.55/person

*Can be made and frozen ahead of time.

Purchase all the products at your wholesale supplier. The half-breasts of chicken are five ounces each and run $.95 each when bought in bulk. They should be baked a month or so in advance and frozen until the big day. The potatoes are canned and are prepared by merely heating in hot margarine and rolling in parsley flakes. They are easily prepared at the last minute.

The beets also come canned, and need to be heated with a little brown sugar to form a glaze. The fruit salad is the same as on the luncheon buffet, except that it is mixed with a little instant pudding mix and served in small compote glasses for a dressier look. The ratio of pudding to fruit salad should be about 1.3 ounces of dry pudding mix to every 7 pounds of fruit salad. Vanilla instant pudding mix is merely dumped, dry from the box, into the fruit salad; the liquid in the fruit salad combines with the mix to give it a creamy thickness. The fruit doesn't need to be drained first because the liquid combines with the mix to cause the thickening process. The red tomato slices, as with the red beets and fruit salad, add needed color to the table.

Hire the Parish Crew
Cost . . . . $8/person, $2,400/300 guests

Many churches provide a kitchen crew who will prepare and serve the reception food. Their menus vary as widely as their beliefs, so you will need to check them out. They serve everything from cold lunchmeat and salad buffets to full sit-down dinners. Some even offer ethnic dishes, such as Swedish Cabbage Rolls or Pepper-cocker Cookies. The $8 per person cost would probably include sliced luncheon meats, cheeses, rolls, mustard, mayonnaise, lettuce, tomato slices, olives, pickles, two types of salad (one pasta and one gelatin), mints, nuts, coffee, tea or punch.

The main advantage of this plan is that it includes all the annoying little extras, such as paper products, tables, linens, serving and cleanup.

Reception Advice

I wish we would have had one of these plans to choose from when we were planning our daughter's reception. The only thing that made sense to us at the time was to find the least expensive caterer possible and order a minimum menu. This is exactly what we did. For a total cost of $3.30 per person we were able to purchase four items: fruit kabobs, chips and dip, pinwheel sandwiches and baby quiche. There was enough food ordered to feed 300 people, but 350 guests actually showed up. Luckily, we had enough of everything but the quiche. (This same caterer, by the way now charges $6.50 per person for this minimum menu.)

The caterers delivered the food and kept the buffet table stocked during the wedding. We did our own setup, cleanup and decorating and we also provided a few small items, including the mints and nuts. If I had it to do again, I would probably choose the "Pro-Am" plan. There were plenty of volunteers at the last minute who would have been happy to bring side dishes. I know you will be better organized than I was by having a ready list of ideas for your volunteers when they ask. Before we go on to the wedding cake, here are some tips on planning your own reception food.

You *must* have someone in charge other than the bride, her mother or members of the wedding party. Preferably, you should have a supervisor and two to three helpers. The best candidates for these volunteer positions are friends or relatives of the bride who have sincerely offered to help in this regard. If you don't have a volunteer to fill this position, call the career placement office at your local college to hire a dependable college student; pay this student well! Even if you have to pay a supervisor $15 or $20 an hour for six hours of work, it will be worth it to you for the thousands of dollars you can save with these economical plans.

The supervisor will keep food on the table by alternating plates. This means that for every food item there is at least one tray on the buffet table and one in the kitchen being refilled. The minute a tray on the buffet table looks "picked at," it needs to be replaced by a fresh one. Then the sloppy one is taken to the kitchen to be added to and "fixed up" for the next replacement. The guests will think you have an endless supply of new food. One of the helpers needs to be the "kitchen magician" who achieves this miracle.

The other helpers should roam among the guests offering any extra food as well as coffee, tea and punch.

You will notice that I always include champagne punch, assuming that you are on a budget and cannot afford the normal one-half bottle of champagne per person, which is what caterers suggest. By adding one full bottle of $5 champagne to each recipe of punch, you can keep the cost of the punch to $.60 per guest, based on two and a half servings each. Here is my very own "secret" punch recipe:

For every 60 servings

Kool-Aid (One can presweetened that makes eight quarts. Make up the eight quarts of Kool-Aid ahead of time by mixing the powder with water according to directions on the can.)	$ 2.07
Sherbet, half gallon	2.25
Generic lemon-lime soda pop, two bottles (two liters each)	1.38
Champagne, one bottle (750 ml)	5.00
Total	$10.70

This will give you fifteen quarts of liquid or sixty servings. The punch can be made with raspberry Kool-Aid and raspberry sherbet, or lime Kool-Aid and lime sherbet, or orange Kool-Aid and orange sherbet. Instead of using regular ice in the punch, which tends to water it down, make ice blocks ahead of time by freezing some of the Kool-Aid in large plastic cups. As you pour the soda pop and champagne onto the dollops of sherbet, the punch will foam and bubble and look *very* expensive. Everyone will want the recipe, but you can just ''play dumb'' if you don't want to divulge the ingredients! I played dumb for years, until now! You, my precious readers, are the first to receive my ''secret recipe.'' Of course, if you wish to skip the champagne, the cost will be even less. By the way, for that special added touch float orange, lemon or lime slices on top.

Creating a Beautiful Buffet Table

My last bit of advice pertains to the ''presentation'' of the buffet table (see page 81). Any caterer or hotel chef will tell you that the most important factor is the way the food appears to the guests. When they walk into the reception hall and see the food, you *must* hear ''ooohs'' and ''aaahs,'' and here are the ways to get them:

1. Fill the table with color for eye appeal. In addition to the colors in the foods, fill in between the dishes with flowers, greenery, ribbons, crepe paper streamers or pyramids of fresh fruit and candles. Close your eyes and try to picture the last time you had Sunday brunch at a nice restaurant. Remember the color and interest tucked in and around the food trays?

2. ''Mirror'' the dishes—that is, have two of every dish, one at each end of the table. This will make it look like ''more.''

3. Elevate the food dishes. *NEVER, NEVER, NEVER* serve trays flat on the table! The difference between your buffet table and a church potluck is the presentation of your food. Place the food on cigar boxes filled with bricks and covered with white linen napkins or a ''staircase'' made out of heavy books covered with a tablecloth. Go crazy with your imagination! Pretend you are a great chef who is being judged on creativity!

4. Garnish the food trays themselves. You don't need to spend hours carving wedding bells out of radishes or love birds out of apples, but you must add something! Here are some ideas:

- ''Frame'' each dish with green leaf lettuce

- Add parsley

- Add huge, fresh strawberries

- Add melon slices, especially bright red watermelon

❧ Add fresh pineapple chunks

❧ Add fresh flowers

I know you will do an amazing job—I wish I could be there to see it!

Create Interesting and Enticing Food Stations

As I mentioned in my Introduction, food stations are the latest trend in reception food service. Each food station is a separate table that serves a certain type of food, such as seafood, prime rib (where a chef stands carving), hors d'oeuvres, fruit and cheese, finger sandwiches, chip and dip, desserts, etc. The reasons why these stations are so trendy are because: they make simple foods seem like "more"; the guests enjoy moving around the room, visiting with other guests who are clustered around the various stations; and many guests can be served at the same time. One bride I know decided to have a dessert reception, and spread food stations around the garden, each with its own specialty dessert. She had a "Chocolate Station," "Sundae and Frozen Yogurt Station," "Pie Station," and a "Custom Crepe Station." By offering all of these desserts, she only needed a small wedding cake.

Of course, in addition to your food stations, you will always need a drink table and a cake table. (By the way, Capaccino and Espresso drinks are becoming popular alternatives to alcoholic beverages.) Coffee and punch may be served from the same drink table or each can have its own table. Quantities vary widely depending on time of day, time of year, type of food, whether it's hot outside or cold. On a warm or hot day when there is icy cold punch, you may not need more than 40-50 cups of coffee. If you have two percolators available, you can always get the second one going while filling your coffee urns from the other, ensuring there is always enough on hand.

The Wedding Cake

The wedding cake is almost as much fun to buy as the wedding gown! I had admired the wedding cakes displayed in bakeries for years, wondering when our daughter would find the right guy. Then the time came—we actually walked into a bakery to price a cake for her real-live wedding! We ordered a four-layer cake that, along with extra sheet cakes served out of the kitchen, would serve at least 250 people. Our total cost came to $185. We could easily have done without the side cakes because only about half the guests wanted dessert. Evidently, this is always true, so don't feel you must provide one serving of cake per guest.

If you haven't priced a wedding cake lately, these are the average costs throughout the country for one that will serve 300 guests:

AREA	TOTAL COST
Northeastern States—Metropolitan	$500
Northeastern States	$450
Southeastern States	$390
Midwestern States	$355
Central Mountain States	$425
Northwestern States	$440
Southwestern States	$500
California—Metropolitan	$500
California	$325

That's the bad news. Now for the money-saving magic. The following ideas will help you cut costs dramatically.

Dummy Cake + Donated Sheet Cakes
Approximate Cost. *$65*

Assemble a "dummy cake" made out of Styrofoam. Have it frosted by an amateur who makes wedding cakes out of her home. Most amateurs I spoke with said they would charge approximately $40 to frost your own cake. Decorate it with your own cake topper or fresh flowers from the supermarket. If you fill the top of each layer with fresh flowers, you can usually get away with frosting the sides yourself. The combination of amateur frosting, supermarket flowers and inexpensive cake top will total about $55; including the cost of the Styrofoam layers, the entire cake will cost about $65. The "dummy cake layers" (actually, rounds of Styrofoam) can be purchased at craft and wedding supply stores. These are the typical prices for two-inch thick "layers":

6″ round	$ 2.29
8″ round	3.25
10″ round	5.09
12″ round	4.69
14″ round	10.75
18″ round	16.05

As long as it is a "fake cake" anyway, you might as well make a big one. Then trail ribbons or cascade more flowers from layer to layer. Of course, you will need to provide one small decorated cake that will sit in back of the large "dummy cake" for the bride and groom to cut during the reception, or you can insert a wedge of real cake into the bottom layer of Styrofoam, frosted over in such a way that only the bride and groom know it's there. Your guests will be amazed! What they won't know is that they are actually being fed donated sheet cakes out of the kitchen, sliced onto little cake plates and served on trays. These sheet cakes will be donated by all those wonderful friends and relatives who ask "if there is anything at all they can do to help." You will need twelve to fifteen sheet cakes cut to feed twenty guests each and they should be the same type of cake—white with white icing, or chocolate with white icing, etc. By the way, you may want to bake a small cake to be used as the top layer, instead of using Styrofoam. That way you'll have it to save and freeze until your first wedding anniversary when you can pull it out and enjoy it with your friends and family.

Dummy Cake + Bake Your Own Sheet Cakes
Approximate Cost. $110

Under this plan you add to the $65 dummy cake sheet cakes that you baked yourself. The cost of the packaged cake mix, oil and eggs for fifteen sheet cakes will be approximately $45. Bake these cakes ahead and freeze them—a really painless process. You will have cakes stored in "volunteer freezers" all over town, but it is worth it.

Buy from a Private Party
Approximate Cost. $175

There are some wonderful cooks out there who make wedding cakes for a living. We have several in our town. One good way to find these jewels is by word-of-mouth; talk to anyone you know who has planned a wedding recently, talk to your club and church friends and, best of all, keep an eye out for cake decorating classes being offered by your local crafts store or community college. These instructors may bake and decorate wedding cakes as a little side business or, if not, they may know of someone who does. In any case, be *sure* to get references.

Buy a Supermarket Cake
Approximate Cost. $150

You will be pleasantly surprised at supermarket bakery prices, which average about $1.00 per serving. I can hardly believe it myself, and I have seen these cakes with my very own eyes. How they can make such a large, beautifully decorated cake for such a low price is beyond me, but definitely worth your consideration. The cake tops are extra, of course, but you can do what we did for our daughter's wedding: decorate the cake yourself with fresh flowers.

Buffet Table Layout

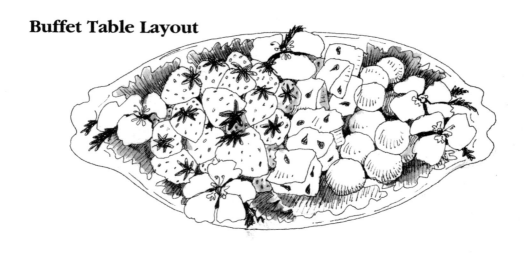

🍒 *Raised tray of finger foods*

Just as important as how the food tastes is how the food looks. An effective buffet presentation will impress your guests and help create an atmosphere of opulence, even on a budget.

Smaller Wedding Cake + Side Cakes
Approximate Cost. **$190**

Order a small wedding cake and a few sheet cakes from a professional bakery.

Affordable Cake Toppers

In addition to the simple idea of adding fresh flowers to your wedding cake, here are some other affordable cake topper ideas:

❦ **Wine Glass With Flowers**
Stand a wine glass on a round mirror for stability; fill it with silk flowers and tufted netting; tie the stem of the glass with a bow and add swirls of tulle netting around the edge of the mirror.

❦ **Tiny White Basket With Flowers**
Use this same idea, only with a basket instead of a wine glass.

❦ **Framed Photo of the Bride and Groom**
The trick to this simple cake topper is to round up an elegant white ceramic or lacy glass frame for the couple's photo; set in on a five-inch by one-inch base of white Styrofoam covered with silk flowers, tufts of white tulle netting and strings of white seed pearls, one of which drapes over an upper corner of the frame.

❦ **Bride and Groom Figurines**
Surely you know someone who collects Precious Moments figurines; ask if you can borrow one of a bride and groom, setting the bisque figurine on a mirror with sprigs of white silk stephanotis sprinkled around the edge of the mirror and at the feet of the bride and groom.

❦ **Blown Glass**
There are dozens of traditional blown glass figures that work just as well, from two hearts entwined, to a wishing well, to a pair of love doves, to a wedding bell suspended from a heart.

❦ **Rotating Music Box**
Borrow a music box that complements your theme; set it on a mirror, surround the base with silk flowers and narrow acetate ribbons and then appoint someone to be in charge of winding the music box off and on during the reception. It will be a real conversation piece!

If you're interested in a few more ideas, including some that require a little bit more time and "crafting ability," such as customized cake toppers to complement your reception theme, you may want to pick up a copy of my book entitled *Beautiful Wedding Decorations and Gifts on a Small Budget.*

Other Food Expenses

Besides the reception food, which is the biggest expense of all, there are other "feedings," as well. The following ideas will help you pull everything together with grace and style.

The Bridesmaids' Luncheon

The bridesmaids' luncheon is traditionally held the Saturday before the wedding. There is sometimes an exchange of gifts at this luncheon. The bridesmaids may give the bride a gift and the bride will probably give each attendant something personal—usually jewelry that can be worn at the wedding.

It is very common for the cost of the luncheon to be shared "dutch treat" by all in attendance, although it may be paid by either the bride or bridesmaids. This little luncheon can be held in a restaurant or a home. It is the duty of the maid or matron of honor to be sure this luncheon date is set.

The Rehearsal Dinner

Lucky for the bride's family—the rehearsal dinner is the responsibility of the groom's family. It has become quite acceptable, however, for those on both sides of the family to "pitch in" and help with this dinner. It can be a spaghetti dinner, an old-fashioned picnic or a barbecue in someone's backyard. Things can get silly after the wedding rehearsal, so there is no need for a formal sit-down dinner; although a member of either family may welcome the opportunity to "entertain" the wedding party with a sit-down dinner in their home dining room. Another good idea is to go "dutch-treat" to a local restaurant where a private room has been reserved. Of course, if the groom's family wishes to have it catered, that's great.

Prewedding Snacks

You will need to provide some kind of nourishment for the nervous wedding party, especially for those who arrive early to dress at the church or synagogue.

If it is a morning wedding, you may want to provide a continental breakfast of coffee, juice and rolls. If the wedding is later in the day, small finger sandwiches are good, as well as cookies and fruit. Just be sure they aren't drippy or messy. This snack should be light, easy and inexpensive. Make things to freeze ahead if you can.

Feed the Musicians, Photographer and Videographer

You will need to provide some kind of nourishment for these contracted workers, although nothing as elaborate or expensive as the food you are serving your guests.

Usually, a simple hot plate or a tray of sandwiches and chips is fine. Provide a separate setting for these workers to take their refreshment.

Feed Those Houseguests!

If ever you don't feel like having houseguests, it's when you are having a wedding, but they come anyway, complete with their party spirit, bubbly enthusiasm and hearty appetites. The best advice I can give you is to go to your friendly wholesale food supplier and buy trays of lasagne. Remember them from the "Pro-Am Combo" plan? You can feed a lot of houseguests for that $11.00. Add to this a salad and some bread.

I hope this chapter has given you some good ideas. I know your notebook is filling with notes and you are making all kinds of decisions! What progress—congratulations! Now, we're ready to tackle the music.

7

And-A-One-And-A-Two . . .

(Affordable Melodies)

Imagine a wedding ceremony and reception without music! How flat! How boring! It would be about as exciting as a nap.

Music is the glue that holds all the pieces together—the flowers and the flounce, the ribbons and the rice, the dress and the "I do's." The strains of the violin or the strum of the guitar—these are the subtle wooings that bring a tear to the eye and a lump to the throat. You may be counting on an organ that shakes the pillars as the bride walks down the aisle on the arm of her dad; and you must have a reception hall that shouts with the same joy being felt by all. But, how will you afford it? And what does it cost, anyway?

If you were one of those writing "a check a day," you would merely arrange for union vocalists at $100 each, a harpist at $150 per hour, and an organist at $110. Then you would hire two ten-piece bands to play during the reception—one with music for the younger generation and one with the classics for the older folks. During the bands' breaks your strolling guitarists would entertain the guests as they nibble on their caviar.

You, however, are on a different kind of budget. Even if you could hire a smaller band, a professional four-piece group for four hours would cost you from $600 to $1,000. Or you might consider a "Mobile Disc Jockey Music Service," also known as a "DJ." This clever person, with complete mixer setup, microphone, and customized sound system, will cost you between $250 and $750 for four hours.

There isn't a regional price breakdown for this chapter because of the tremendous variation in musicians' fees within each region of the country. When we are dealing with artists, the fees depend upon their reputation and not their location.

I do, however, have plenty of cost-cutting ideas, which are explained on the next several pages.

Cutting the Cost of Ceremony Music

Free Recital
No Cost $0

Under this plan your musically talented friends and relatives donate all the music, both vocally and instrumentally. You probably have much more talent in your family and circle of acquaintances than you even realize. Ask around and you may find that your niece plays the harp beautifully in her school orchestra, or that your cousin is an accomplished flautist. A word of caution: the music is one of the most important contributions to the mood of your day and you certainly don't want an embarrassingly shaky performance, so you may want to stage a discreet audition. In any case, ask for recommendations from others who have heard the performances. You will also need someone who can play the organ or piano and one or two vocalists.

Pro-Am Combo
Approximate Cost. *$40*

Hire one professional, such as the church organist, and then use the same kind of talent discussed under the "Free Recital" plan for the rest of the ceremony. An excellent organist is sometimes the most difficult to find and you may have to pay for one's services. Nothing is more disconcerting than a novice who makes the church organ sound like a carnival calliope, but by hiring the church organist you will pay much less than a union musician provided by a professional agency.

On the other hand, you may have an accomplished organist in the family, but not a single person who can sing in public without trembling. In this case, use the free organist and splurge on a local vocalist who sings at weddings for a "nonprofessional" fee. You can find these talented people by talking to past brides or to the head of the Music Department of your local university, who will be happy to recommend outstanding music students who not only need the experience, but the extra money as well. After all, even a "Big Mac," fries and Coke dig into a student's meager budget.

Canned and Fresh
Approximate Cost. *$40*

Use "canned music," via cassette tape, combined with a real live $40 vocalist who will sing to a taped accompaniment. The cassette tape will have prerecorded music that you have selected. The music will be in the order of the ceremony, beginning with the seating of the guests and ending with the recessional. Your public library has records and tapes of suitable music. Check them out and record them onto your ceremony tape. Be sure that the library's copy is in excellent shape with no scratches or skips. If necessary, invest in a new copy of the album to assure high quality. When recording onto your ceremony tape, use very high fidelity recording equipment. You certainly don't want the wedding march to sound muddy or tinny. If your own recording equipment is inferior for this purpose, find an audiophile friend who will make this recording for you on high-quality, state-of-the-art equipment.

This plan obviously requires a volunteer to start and stop the tape which, preferably, will be played over the church's sound system.

All Local Talent
Approximate Cost. *$120*

Hire three nonunion musicians at $40 each. In addition to an organist, you will probably need one vocalist and one other instrumentalist. These nonprofessional people are available locally and frequently perform at weddings. You may discover them when you hear them perform at a church or another wedding. Ask for suggestions from other brides and, again, check with the university music department.

Cutting the Cost of Reception Music

Free Recital
No Cost. *$0*

Just as with the ceremony, the "Free Recital" musicians are your talented relatives and friends. You will find that the reception lends itself even more to available talent because the music is usually less formal than the ceremony music. The ceremony requires a little more expertise, mainly due to its more classical music, but the reception opens itself up to all kinds of popular music. Sniff around for a talented band or singing group. Who knows, a folk guitarist or jazz pianist may be sitting in your living room right this minute! Put on your thinking cap and ask everyone you know. Your reception can be filled with fabulously entertaining music if you can only find the musicians and it isn't difficult to do. Our society is loaded with lawyers, nurses, teachers and secretaries who also happen to be musically talented. Pretend you are a talent scout—go out and find them!

Piped-In Music
No Cost. *$0*

This idea is too good to be true—free music available over the sound system. Many halls have background music that is already programmed and ready to use. Ask when you reserve your reception site. There are so many wonderful tracks available these days, but if the music is the "elevator" variety, you won't be interested. Be sure to listen to it ahead of time!

Amateur DJ
No Cost. *$0*

Do you realize how many young people there are out there who own their own DJ equipment? They may have worked two paper routes at once, plus mowed lawns on Saturdays to get all this stuff, and they are dying to use it in public. If you doubt that, just think of the kids who drive around with their speakers blaring. The capacity of their speakers will even shake you out of a sound sleep. It seems obvious to me that the owners of these systems need an audience, and what better audience than the guests at your reception! Find a guy or gal who is outgoing enough to actually use the microphone, serving as your Master of Ceremonies. Just to be safe, ask friends if they know of anyone they can recommend, because you will need one who is mature enough to take direction, especially when it comes to choice of music.

You will need help rounding up the kind of music you want played, but between your own library and that of the amateur DJ, you will come up with plenty of ideas. Listen to any music recommended by your DJ friend to be sure it is suitable. For anything you lack, borrow it from your local public library, including any ethnic or specialty music you may need, such as the Hora, the polka or the tango. One suggestion: because your volunteer friend is doing this service strictly for fun, be sure to have one or two "relief DJs" who can fill in so that they can all enjoy the reception.

Party Tapes
No Cost $0

This plan is similar to the last one, except that the music is provided on a series of one-hour cassette tapes that have been prerecorded with your own selection of music. Take time in the weeks before the wedding to transfer music from records and tapes (including ethnic and specialty numbers) onto the reception tapes. Number them in order and have someone who will play them continually. You can even have the bride and groom's first dance music recorded onto the beginning of one of the tapes.

Again, this will require a dependable volunteer. The volume can be adjusted from loud to soft, depending on whether you need the music for dancing or background.

Two for One Sale
Approximate Cost. $75

Hire the same person to be the organist at the ceremony and the pianist at the reception. It costs less to hire one person to perform at both functions than to hire two separate musicians. Most organists also play the piano very well, but this is only a suggestion—you may know an organist who is talented on a number of other instruments, giving you a choice.

All Local Talent
Approximate Cost. $200

For this amount of money, you can hire one or two vocalists or one or two instrumentalists. You could also hire a small band composed of local students or a string trio or brass quartet. Keep your eyes and ears open when you attend other functions. The talent is out there and you can find it.

The music for our daughter's wedding cost $185. We had three musicians at $40 each, including the church pianist and organist, a vocalist who accompanied herself on the guitar at $40 and two soloists, one of whom donated her services. The other charged $25.

The ceremony music was classical with a flute/harpsichord duet, piano and organ music, a vocal solo and a vocal duet. The only reception music that we paid for was the tearjerker, "Sunrise, Sunset," from *Fiddler on the Roof,* sung by a wonderful soprano who accompanied herself on the guitar. She sang the song to accompany a touching slide presentation showing the bride and groom from babyhood to engagement. There weren't too many dry eyes!

Musical Advice

Because you are your own wedding consultant, these are some things you should know about planning the music:

1. Always check with the clergyman or rabbi before planning the ceremony music. There are various rules you may need to follow. Some religious denominations, for example, don't approve of the traditional wedding march. Others will not allow any secular music at all. You will also need permission to use the sound system.

2. Ask a church organist for musical ideas for the ceremony.

3. Be careful that you don't use music as a "filler" or mere entertainment during the ceremony. The ceremony music should be selected because of its solemnity.

4. Familiarize yourself with the traditional music usually played or sung during a wedding ceremony. This will help you make your selections, even if you do deviate from the norm. Our daughter, for instance, chose the "Wedding March" from *The Sound of Music* for her recessional.

These are three common prelude selections you will discover in your research:

> "Arioso" by Bach
>
> "Larghetto" by Handel
>
> "Adagio" by Liszt

Two favorite processionals are:

> "Aria in F Major" by Handel
>
> "March in C" by Purcell

If you want to be in royal company, you may select Lady Di's processional music:

"Trumpet Voluntary" by Jeremiah Clarke

Here are some of the traditional love songs sung during the ceremony:

"The Greatest of These Is Love" by Bitgood

"O Perfect Love" by Barnby

"I Love Thee" by Grieg

If you decide to break the classical tradition, here are more modern love songs:

"Follow Me" by John Denver

"We've Only Just Begun" by Roger Nichols

"Hawaiian Wedding Song" by Al Hoffman and Dick Manning

"All I Ask of You" from *The Phanton of the Opera* by Webber, Hart and Stiltoe

"Evergreen" by Streisand and Williams

"Wedding Song" by Paul Stookey

"Do You Remember?" by J. Ivanovici

"Morning Has Broken" by Eleanor Farjeon

"What I Did for Love" by Marvin Hamlisch

Anything goes at the reception, but here are some of the most popular "first dances" for the bride and groom:

"Unforgettable" by Irving Gordon

"Wonderful Tonight" by Eric Clapton

"Looking Through the Eyes of Love" by Hamlisch and Sager

"Can You Feel the Love Tonight?" by John and Rice

"Just the Way You Are" by Billy Joel

"Endless Love" by Diana Ross and Lionel Ritchie

"Stand by Me" by Ben E. King

"I'll Always Love You" by Taylor Dane

Here are some of the most popular father-daughter and mother-son dance selections. For the father-daughter dance:

"My Heart Belongs to Daddy" by Cole Porter

"Sunrise, Sunset" from *Fiddler on the Roof* by Harnick and Bock

"Thank Heaven for Little Girls" from *Gigi* by Lerner and Loewe

"My Girl" by Robinson and White

"The Times of Your Life" by Paul Anka

For the mother-son dance

"You Are the Sunshine of My Life" by Stevie Wonder

"Wind Beneath My Wings" by Silbar and Henley

"Summer Wind" by Mayer and Mercer

"My Mother's Eyes" by Gilbert and Baer

All these musical suggestions are given to inspire you to research for yourself. Go to your local music store and thumb through some wedding songbooks—you'll have no difficulty narrowing your choice to those precious selections that will give your day special beauty and meaning. Just beware of one thing: if you decide to use "Sunrise, Sunset," add a case of Kleenex to your shopping list!

8

Clever, Cute and Crafty

(Ambiance on a Budget)

The decorations require a creative spirit, a wild imagination and a wide open mind; this is the one place where you may decide to break away from tradition completely. Following your theme, the decorations will establish a certain "feeling" or ambiance during the ceremony and reception. The theme is determined by two things: the degree of formality you would like and the availability of decorative items you can borrow, rent, purchase or make inexpensively.

If you were one of the "check-a-day" people, you wouldn't be concerned about cost because money can buy ambiance. However, you are on a small budget, so you will need an extra special "thinking cap" in order to come up with ideas that are "creative" and "cheap" at the same time—and that can make your brain hurt! Are you ready to take on the challenge? Great! Here's the signal—"Go for it!"

First of all, let's clarify what I mean by *ambiance.* You will have a better picture of the meaning after you hear the stories of two recent weddings. The mood, or ambiance, was very different in each case.

The first wedding was held two days after Christmas in the evening. The theme was a "Magical Forest" created by the use of a darkened sanctuary and reception hall, dozens of evergreen trees, tiny white lights, and candles. When the usher seated me for the ceremony there was a hush over the congregation as we sat in the darkness. Our eyes adjusted quickly and then we could see that the sanctuary was filled with evergreen trees and boughs. Even the platform was loaded with trees dressed in tiny white lights, and candles glowed on artistically placed candelabras.

A talented classical pianist played softly—the piano was the only musical instrument used throughout the ceremony. The concept was really very simple, and yet it set an elegant and sanctified mood. When the bride came down the aisle to the strains of more classical music, she looked like the "dream princess" of her magical forest. She wore a sophisticated satin dress accented with silver sequins that reflected the subtle lights. No one dared breathe; it was as if we were characters in a fairy tale.

The same ambiance prevailed at the reception. Even the hallway that joined the sanctuary and reception site was dark except for light-covered trees that lined it. As the guests walked from the sanctuary to the reception, they spoke in whispers. We squinted as we entered the hall lined with more delicately lighted trees. There was a single white candle in the center of each round table where hors d'oeuvres were served. The pianist was already at the grand piano and the same quiet classical music continued. Again, everyone spoke very softly and when I left, it felt as if I were walking out of a dream back into reality.

Even though the mood for this wedding and reception was one of royal elegance, it had been created by the use of leftover trees that had practically been given away by frustrated Christmas tree vendors (the wedding was two days after Christmas, remember), candles bought by the gross, and borrowed Christmas tree lights. And, look at the result—a wonderful example of an expensive look on a tight budget!

The second wedding had an opposite mood. It was a happy, loud, colorful, daytime wedding with a frolicking, festive reception. The sanctuary was decorated with several dozen grapevine wreaths, including two enormous ones that hung in back of the platform. They were wrapped with ribbons and dotted with bright flowers and natural greenery from a "free florist." The candles and pew boughs were bright lavender and peach. The organ was as tastefully loud and cheerful as were the bridesmaids' dresses. I would call the sanctuary theme "Happy Springtime!"

The reception was a grand party, using a circus theme with a master of ceremonies dressed up like a circus master. There were clowns, a balloon sculptor and a mime. The bright wedding colors were repeated with the use of crepe paper, balloons and a "big top" made from plain brown butcher paper hung from the ceiling.

The guests were animated and good-humored, all because of the deliberate use of "things" that created the festive atmosphere. And none of these things were expensive. The bride and her sister made all the grapevine wreaths for the sanctuary, starting from scratch with actual grapevines from the San Joaquin Valley in California. They covered them with inexpensive ribbons and free flowers. The reception plans were made based on the availability of friends who agreed to perform as circus master, mime and balloon sculptor. Meanwhile, the crepe paper, balloons (nonhelium variety) and tent top were very inexpensive.

The contrasting settings of these two weddings demonstrate the importance of a theme. The first wedding and reception had a traditional theme, while the second deviated from the norm with its rollicking party atmosphere. The important thing to remember is that, vague or specific, traditional or not, you *must have some kind of theme.* The theme is the skeleton that will support your plans; it affects every decision you will make, from the wedding colors to the length of the gowns and from the melodies to the cake top. Choose your theme carefully; it should not be used as a gimmick, but as a true reflection of the personalities of the bride and groom.

I spoke with a photographer who has done hundreds of weddings and he said that ethnic weddings are so much fun they make the rest seem awfully boring. I tend to agree; the rest of us need to come up with a special theme to spice things up. So, if you have an ethnic background, take advantage of it when planning your wedding, even if the traditions haven't been passed down in your family. What proud and wonderful traditions you have—rekindle as many as possible by incorporating them into your ceremony and reception.

What could be more precious than watching the Mexican bride and groom being wrapped with a white cord, symbolizing their union? Or the Greek couple being connected by matching crowns? Often their crowns are made of orange blossoms from the orange tree, a symbol of fertility, bearing golden fruit, sweet-scented white flowers and leaves all at once. Jacqueline Kennedy and Aristotle Onassis were crowned with orange blossoms in their traditional Greek ceremony in 1968.

Crowns, in fact, are part of many ethnic ceremonies, including the Eastern Orthodox wedding where the bride and groom each wear a gold crown. After the wedding a Finnish bride holds her crown in her hands as she is blindfolded; while girls dance around her in a circle, she places the crown on the head of one of the dancing girls, who is said to be the next to marry.

The Jewish bridegroom breaks a glass at the end of the wedding ceremony to call to mind the incompleteness of all rejoicing as long as the temple in Jerusalem remains in ruins.

Research your own heritage and use it as your theme. Meanwhile, the rest of us "homogenized" Americans need lots of help to keep things interesting. The following ideas should help you get started, but don't be limited by them. Give your imagination a free rein and you'll be amazed at what you come up with!

Wedding reception themes often employ garden imagery, probably because weddings were traditionally scheduled in June; however, garden themes will work wonderfully year 'round. Here are a few:

Traditional Themes

A Rose Garden

Fill the reception hall with as many roses as you can find. Borrow potted and cut roses from friends and relatives. What you lack, buy in silks from your Oriental import outlet or favorite craft store. Be sure to buy them in "bush" form which will give you more roses for the money. Cover the pots with paper in the wedding colors and tie with ribbons.

When you have borrowed or bought all the roses possible, fill the rest of the room with any other greenery you can find, including potted shrubs, trees or garlands made from any natural greenery from the "free florist."

Once you have created the garden, set wrought iron or old-fashioned park benches among the greenery. Finish off the look with borrowed birdbaths. Stand pots of flowers in the birdbaths, or fill them with water and float rose petals and candles on top.

Hearts and Flowers

Use borrowed greenery of all kinds, dotted with flowers. The flowers can be any variety, but they should all be wrapped with paper and ribbons in the wedding colors.

Cut hearts out of posterboard. The hearts should be in two sizes—six-inch and three-inch—and they should be in the primary wedding color. Use ribbons to hang them from the borrowed greenery; scatter them among the colorful flowers.

Use flowers as filler on the buffet table and place helium-filled heart-shaped balloons all over the hall. Tie them on the backs of chairs; tape them to the sides of the cake table.

Summer in the Park

We are back to a garden-type setting again; this time the emphasis is on the wrought iron benches, birdbaths and the addition of old street lamps. If you can borrow only one of these decorative lamps, it will help set the mood.

Use the greenery ideas from the "Rose Garden" theme and the mixed flower ideas from the "Hearts and Flowers" theme. Add a "flower cart," whether real or pretend. It can be filled with flowers and trailed with ribbons.

Is this giving you some ideas? Here are some other traditional themes:

Paris in Springtime	Romantic Candlelight
Cupid and Love Doves	Autumn Harvest
Victorian Tea Party	Christmas Joy
Ice Palace	Valentine's Day
Winter Wonderland	

Every one of the ceremony themes, mentioned later in this chapter, can also be used for the reception. This would make it easy, in fact, because you would only need to come up with one theme to carry throughout the wedding and reception.

Next we come to the nontraditional "party theme" ideas. These may not appeal to you at first, but you should definitely be aware of them just in case you decide to break tradition.

Nontraditional Themes

Louisiana Plantation Theme

Decorate with silk magnolia blossoms, gazebos, trellises and "parasols" (old umbrellas covered with crepe paper). The hostesses could wear Southern belle dresses and the getaway car could be a horse and carriage.

Mexican Fiesta Theme

Decorate with all the colorful and festive Mexican things you can find—huge crepe paper flowers, serapes, pinatas, the works! Do you have any friends who can play Mariachi music? If not, records are available at your public library.

Polynesian Theme

This works well around a swimming pool. Include Hawaiian music, of course, and maybe even hula dancers. Then add Tiki torches, conch shells, Hawaiian fabrics, flower leis and colorful crepe paper flowers and garlands. Create "environmental" background music by playing records or tapes of real ocean sounds. Complete the scene by floating rafts of fresh or crepe paper flowers in the pool and filling your buffet table with as much Polynesian fare as you can afford: roast pork, fresh pineapple, fresh coconut, grilled fish, melons, strawberries, loaves of sweet Hawaiian bread, sweet potatoes and, of course, bowls of poi (everyone loves to complain how it tastes like wallpaper paste!). Do you know anyone who can sing the Hawaiian Wedding Song?

Nostalgia Theme

Fill the reception site with memorabilia from the couple's past: baby photos; school awards; Little League uniform; cheerleading uniform; pom-poms; copies of their high school and college yearbooks; dress up the couple's actual childhood teddy bears (if they still exist) as bride and groom. As you gather things from the bride's and groom's childhood and school years, more ideas will come to you, including something clever for the cake top: miniature megaphones with their school emblem? Tiny teddy bears dressed as bride and groom or, perhaps dressed as cheerleader and football player? Use your imagination.

A Country-Western Roast

You can carry this theme as far as you like, decorating with lariats, cowboy hats, saddles, branding irons, single-trees, red bandanas, potted cactus plants and bales of hay. Cover your tables with checkered tablecloths and hire a country-western band or a country singer or play taped music. Give your reception a roast theme in every sense of the word, from barbecued foods to stand-up comedy as several friends and family members "roast" the bride and groom, using family photos, home movies, videos and true stories of embarrassing incidents. This idea works best for an informal outdoor reception in a park, in someone's oversized backyard or, ideally, at a real farm or ranch. One bride even went so far as to make paper mache cowboy-boot centerpieces, miniature cowboy-hat favors filled with trail mix, and a "lasso-wrapped" wedding cake. As the coup de grace, see if you can round up a horse-drawn hay wagon as your getaway vehicle.

Balloon Theme

The simple use of balloons, whether helium-filled or not, can create a stunning ambiance all by themselves. Here are some clever ways to decorate with balloons:

❦ Bouquets

Add bouquets of helium-filled balloons throughout your reception site, as table centerpieces, colorful fillers "growing" up from the floor, tied to the backs of chairs or along bannisters or railings, in windowsills, over doorways, to frame the bride and groom at the cake table or in the receiving line, or to create a "walkway" for the couple and their attendants to use as they enter the reception hall.

❦ *Archways*

Helium balloons, when attached to a fishing line held down at each end with heavy bricks, will form a natural arch by themselves! In fact with no help from you at all, they will actually *insist* on arching at the center, a convenient law of physics that will enable you to create archways over the head table, the receiving line, the cake table, or for the guests or wedding party to walk under as they enter the reception hall.

❦ *Cover the Ceiling*

Attach one helium-filled balloon to one regular balloon, tie them together with crinkle tie ribbon at their nipples, leaving several feet dangling down. Then, release them and let them float to the ceiling; when the reception is over and it is time for the bride and groom to make their escape, invite each guest to "catch" one to take outside and release into the sky as the couple drives away.

Fifties Theme

Decorate the reception hall with fifties memorabilia, including Elvis posters, photographs of the parents or other relatives in their prom outfits or pictures of vintage fifties cars. Have a disc jockey do a "Wolf Man Jack" impression while playing fifties music. Top it off with a 1956 Cadillac convertible as the getaway car, trailing old shoes and tin cans. If you can't find a Cadillac, a '56 Chevy will do!

Are you getting the hang of it? Here are a few more theme party reception ideas:

Gay nineties	Mississippi Riverboat
Roaring twenties	A Ship's Cruise
Renaissance Festival	Hollywood Movie Set
Tropical Rain Forest	Mountain Ski Resort
Carousel Horses	Beach Party
Happy New Year	

Ceremony Themes

A ceremony theme is usually more formal than the reception theme, although it may be carried over to the reception if you would like. Here are some of the more popular ceremony themes:

Costume Wedding

Costume weddings are very trendy these days. All you need is a theme that lends itself to costumes, such as: Henry VIII English Tudor; Renaissance; Medieval; Folk; Halloween; Masked Ball; Western; Polynesian; Guys 'n Dolls; Romeo & Juliet; Elizabethan; Victorian; Edwardian; Greco-Roman; Southern Antebellum; or any ethnic theme.

Costumes for these weddings may be sewn from patterns, rented from costume shops, borrowed from theatrical production companies, rented or purchased through catalogs available at many bridal salons.

Snowball Wedding

This is a wedding where all the women wear white, including the mothers and grandmothers, which projects a very elegant look to the ceremony. The men wear black tuxedos or white dinner jackets with black trousers. You may choose to decorate with white flowers and ribbon, as well, and include all-white bouquets for the women and boutonnieres for the men; however, I much prefer one dramatic shock of color splashed against the white, such as bright pink roses interspersed among the white arrangements with perhaps a touch of matching pink ribbon. It is a matter of personal taste, but the important thing is this: It is *imperative* that all the whites match! If they don't, the off-whites or ivories will appear to be dingy or dirty and the entire effect will be ruined. The smart thing is to let the bride select her gown first and match all the other whites to it, including the flowers, pew bows, candles, hairpieces and even the aisle runner, if you choose to use one.

Black-and-White Wedding

All the wedding costumes are black and/or white. The men may wear black tuxes, the attendants black gowns with white trim, the flower girl white and the ring bearer black, for example. This is a very popular 1990s theme, but be sure there is a little color splashed around somewhere or the wedding will lose its festive feeling. By the way, it is also popular for the bride's attendants to choose individual dresses of their choice, just so they are black and white. This same idea works for a Navy Blue-and-White Wedding, as well.

Christmas Wedding

This is an easy theme to work with because of all the Christmas trees, holly, poinsettias and evergreenery available in December. Also, it's only natural to take advantage of all the tiny white Christmas tree lights that abound during the season, stringing them everywhere, creating a magical touch of winter wonderland.

Victorian Wedding

You can carry the Victorian theme as far as you like—all the way to period costumes and high-buttoned shoes if that appeals to you. Be sure to include plenty of lace, hearts, trailing ribbons, and you may want to create old-fashioned tussie-mussie bouquets for the bride and her attendants (a tussie mussie is a small cluster of flowers, tied with ribbons and tucked into an elegant cone-shaped holder.)

Candlelight Wedding

Plan an evening wedding that incorporates as many candles as you can afford, mounted on pillars, in candelabra, along windowsills and altar railings, on tall candlesticks at the end of every other pew, and atop the organ and piano. Have your bridal attendants carry a single candle imbedded in an oasis filled with fresh flowers and, of course, include a traditional unity candle behind the altar. If you carry this theme through to your reception, you may want to give decorated candles as "favors" for the guests to light as you leave the reception, creating a glowing, romantic pathway from the reception site to your getaway vehicle.

The Home Wedding

More and more brides are choosing to be married at home in the presence of a limited number of friends and family members, followed by a large reception at another site. The nice thing about a home wedding is that the natural charm and intimacy of the home itself offers a romantic ambiance for the wedding; also, a home setting takes very little in the way of decorations. The first step is to unclutter the rooms: remove the oversized pieces of furniture (even if you only store them in the garage for the big day), and clear away most of the nicknacks, family photos, etc. This will leave room for white folding chairs, if you choose to use them, and a few small flower arrangements. The fireplace mantle may be decorated with greens, flowers, candles and ribbons and an altar can be created easily by covering any small table with a lace or damask tablecloth. By the way, if the room is too small for chairs, it is perfectly acceptable for the guests to stand during the ceremony. If you are marrying in the summer, you may decide to have the ceremony in the garden of your home, simplifying things all the more: you won't need any floral decorations; no heavy furniture to move; and no clutter to clear away.

An Indoor Garden Wedding

If you have your heart set on a garden wedding, but you are getting married in the winter, or you can't come up with an available garden for your ceremony, create the illusion of a garden indoors. This is easier than you might think. For starters, rent or borrow as much greenery as you can find (silk or fresh), from potted silk ficus trees, to potted patio shrubs and plants, to hanging fuchsia baskets, to ordinary house plants. As I have already mentioned, many nurseries will loan out or rent a designated number of potted bushes or trees for local weddings, but also scour the homes and patios of your close friends and family members, and while you're at it, keep an eye out for any portable trellises, arbors and white wrought iron benches or attractive wicker or white plastic patio furniture. If you can't round up arbors and trellises, they are available for rent at wedding supply stores, along with white picket fences, which really add a country garden ambiance to the setting. Next, wind silk or fresh ivy and flowers around these props, tie them with bows and you'll have a lovely garden, regardless of the season. This is one of the easiest and most affordable themes, by the way.

Here are a few more theme possibilities:

Basket of Flowers	Hearts
Wreaths	Flower Garden
Bells	Apple Blossoms
Golden Rings	Candles and Harps
Garden Trellises	Doves
Rose-Covered Arches	Parasols

For even more theme ideas, pick up a copy of my new book entitled *Beautiful Wedding Decorations and Gifts on a Small Budget.*

Cost-Cutting Decorations

For our daughter's wedding and reception we came up with a "Winter Wonderland" theme. As I mentioned in the chapter on flowers, we used pine boughs from the "free florist" in the sanctuary and we also took advantage of Christmas decorations already provided by the church, including an enormous tree covered with thousands of white lights. The reception hall was filled with evergreen trees and shrubs loaned to us by a local nursery, along with pine boughs we strung together and draped everywhere we could. We trimmed all the trees and tables with large and small burgundy bows.

The ambiance was mainly created by the free trees and shrubs, so our "big" expense was a $50 "ice sculpture" burgundy swan that became the centerpiece for the buffet table. We special-ordered this from the caterer, and it was a big hit. It sat in a bed of crushed ice that we covered with flowers from the produce department of the local supermarket. These flowers, by the way, cost a fraction of what they would cost at the retail florist and were very convenient for last-minute purchases. I have learned since the wedding that ice sculptures are easy to make with do-it-yourself plastic molds that can be purchased at wholesale food suppliers. We could have made the same molded swan for only $32 if we had known.

Our main expenses in the sanctuary were the pew bows, which I made for $.70 each, and candles, $.49 each. The church had candle holders and sconces already affixed to the sanctuary walls and pillars. By the way, it takes a one-hundred-yard roll of two-inch acetate ribbon to make ten large pew bows. Each roll costs about $7.

Our total expense for decorating the church and reception hall came to approximately $110. Everything else was borrowed or from the "free florist."

Your total expenses can be even lower than this by selecting a theme that uses things freely available to you. Of course, you must select a theme that reflects the personalities of the bride and groom; however, if you have several in mind, select the one that will help your pocketbook. Train your eye to look for the following:

Traditional Themes

Wrought-iron or wooden benches

Nice lawn furniture (especially wicker)

Trellises

Latticework

Portable gazebos

Potted plants

Potted flowers (especially roses)

Potted shrubs, topiaries, trees

Bells of all types

Hearts

Love doves

Baskets

Dried grapevines

Wreaths of artificial flowers

Umbrellas of all sizes

Nontraditional Themes

Tiki torches

Old-fashioned decorative streetlamps

Varied lighting, including strings of patio lights

Chinese lanterns

Posters

Wall hangings

Tropical plants

Sleighbells

Skiis, snowshoes, sleds

Wooden shoes, small windmills, potted tulips

Old South memorabilia

Gay nineties memorabilia

Fifties memorabilia

Costumes of all kinds

Antique clothes of all kinds

Of course, it would take an entire book to cover this subject thoroughly, but this will give you an idea. Just remember in the wedding calendar suggested in chapter two, the actual reception plans don't need to be made until five months before the wedding. If your reception needs to be planned in less time, you will need to select a theme that lends itself to things you already have on hand or can easily obtain. Otherwise, five months should give you time to watch for these things, and anything else you see that is *moveable*! You will undoubtedly come up with ideas of your own—it's a wonderfully creative challenge!

As an example, you may have a loving and adoring aunt and uncle with a Shangri-la backyard full of archways, trellises, wrought-iron park benches, elegant lawn furniture, portable pots of flowers, trees and shrubs, strings of Victorian patio lights, hanging flower baskets and several decorative streetlamps. Depending on just how loving and adoring they are, you may have your entire reception decor right there. If not, they may be happy to loan you a good part of it. See how it works? All you need are

How to Tie Pew Bows

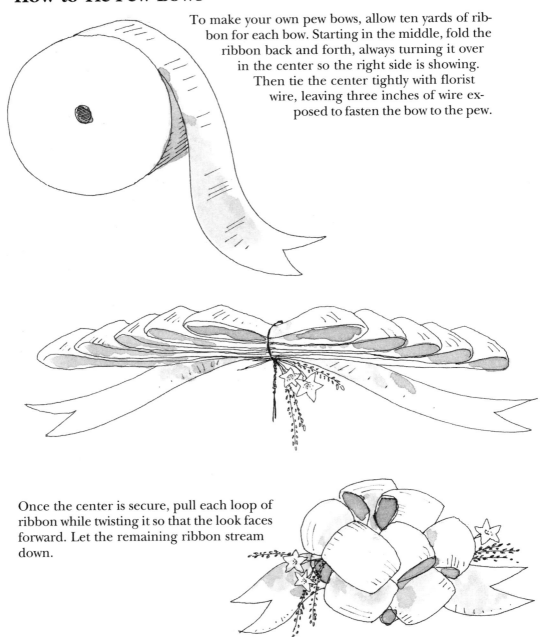

To make your own pew bows, allow ten yards of ribbon for each bow. Starting in the middle, fold the ribbon back and forth, always turning it over in the center so the right side is showing. Then tie the center tightly with florist wire, leaving three inches of wire exposed to fasten the bow to the pew.

Once the center is secure, pull each loop of ribbon while twisting it so that the look faces forward. Let the remaining ribbon stream down.

some contributions to the cause—and don't forget my advice from chapter five: "look as pitiful as possible when you ask." In fact, if you look extra-pitiful, they may suggest having the reception in their yard!

Another source of ideas are garage sales. It is always amazing to me to see what people are trying to sell at these things, especially if they are moving.

You can always rent a little ambiance, too. Here are some typical rental prices for things that may help:

White picket fencing, 2 × 4 feet	$ 2.75 ea.
Lattice trellis	65.00
Lattice screens	35.00
Urns	10.00/pair
Wishing well	10.00
Kneeling bench	16.00
Gazebo	125.00
Canopy, 20 × 20 feet	195.00
Carousel horses	35.00
Garden tables and umbrellas	19.50
Mirror ball with lights	35.00
Dance floors, 12 × 15 feet	160.00
Helium tanks for filling balloons (will fill three hundred large balloons)	30.00
Champagne fountain	35.00
White plastic folding chairs	.60 ea.
Pillars	15.00/pair
Flowers urns	15.00/pair
9-light candelabra	22.00/pair
Large white bird cage	15.00
9-foot white, free-standing umbrella	28.00
Decorated wedding arch	27.00
Money tree	7.00
White canopy, 20 × 20 feet	165.00

After you have borrowed or rented everything you can, you will still need to purchase a few things. Here is a sample shopping list:

Crepe paper streamers, 500 feet	$ 6.25
Crepe paper sheets	2.50
Candles, 12"	.50 ea.
Candles, 18"	.80 ea.
Ice molds	32.00
Balloons, helium	.90 ea.
Balloons, regular (package of 100)	.10 ea.
2" Ribbon, 100 yards	9.25
1" Ribbon, 100 yards	5.50
Posterboard	.90
Grapevine wreaths, undecorated	6.75

If you are very clever, your actual purchases shouldn't total more than $200. Believe me, you can have all the ambiance you can handle for even less than that. Keep thinking "free" and "borrowed"—and keep your "thinking cap" handy!

9

Say Cheese!

(Capture the Memories at Affordable Prices)

The day after the wedding can be a depressing letdown to the families of the bride and groom. The cake is a memory, the guests have gone home and the flowers are as tired as the mother of the bride. There is a delightful cure, however, for these post-wedding blues: the moments captured in photos and videotape.

A videotape of the wedding and reception will bring instant delight. Even as the loving couple enjoys their honeymoon, families and friends can be reliving the happy day. And since it doesn't have to be processed, videotape can be replayed immediately. If you have a VCR, you can settle back in your easy chair and enjoy the results of all your successful planning.

The photographs require more time because they must be processed and printed, but they, too, will capture the memories. The average cost of wedding photography in this country is close to $1,000.

You will probably want to record your special day in both ways, and that is where the problem arises because photo and video packages can be very costly.

I priced videography packages all over the United States and I found that the costs did not vary so much from state to state as from company to company. Wedding videography is a relatively new field, and there do not seem to be measurable standards. A typical videotape plan, however, consisted of one camera and one videographer for two hours, no editing provided. This plan ranged from $250 to $1,000.

By adding a second camera and videographer, the cost can go up as much as $500. Other extras include: a photo montage of baby pictures, interviews at the reception, a highlight tape at the end, a visit to the home on the day of the wedding, special editing, graphics and commentary. Each of these special services adds an additional $100 to $500 to the overall cost.

Photography prices throughout the United States seemed to settle into more of a pattern. There can be extreme highs and lows among still photographers in any given city, but these are the costs for a bride's average package consisting of four 8×10's, forty 4×5's and a leather album. The parents' package includes twelve 5×7's in a vinyl album.

AREA	PARENTS'	BRIDE'S
Northeastern States—Metropolitan	$425	$1,050
Northeastern States	$375	$ 900
Southeastern States	$350	$ 600
Midwestern States	$200	$ 650
Central Mountain States	$250	$ 500
Northwestern States	$320	$ 800
Southwestern States	$300	$ 950
California—Metropolitan	$375	$1,000
California	$250	$ 750

Most of these photographers will provide approximately 150 proofs from which the bride and her parents will select. The actual cost to the photographer of each proof, including film and processing, averages $1. This means that 150 shots will cost the photographer approximately $150. There are other expenses, of course, such as equipment and overhead, but the main chunk of money is going toward the photographer's labor. I have several ways for you to cut costs on both photography and videography. Let's begin with the photographer.

Cost-Cutting Photography Plans

Amateur Photographer
Approximate Cost. $120

Under this plan, we are assuming you have a friend or relative who takes pretty good pictures, has the right kind of camera and, most important, agrees to photograph your wedding for free. The $120 will cover the film, developing, and printing of approximately 144 pictures. A roll of thirty-six-exposure, color print film for a 35mm camera will cost about $5.75. The developing of this film, plus printing of 5×7's, will cost approximately $30 per roll, depending on whether you have them processed at a drugstore or photo lab. You must have the entire roll of film printed in 5×7's at the time of the processing or the price will be much higher.

These 5×7's can serve as proofs as well as photos for your album. If anyone wants to have certain pictures printed up in larger sizes, they can order these later. A 16×20 will cost about $25, for example, if ordered from a quality photo lab. Drugstore processing labs are much less expensive, but not as desirable for the larger sizes. But even if no one orders enlargements, there will probably be at least 100 of the 144 shots taken that will turn out well enough to be used in the bride's and parents' albums. The parents may even want to contribute toward a double print order, which will provide twice as many prints. The albums themselves can be purchased later.

Be sure your amateur photographer has a quality camera with features at least as good as those listed under the "Rented Camera" plan. If the camera is a 35mm, I recommend using Kodak Ektar, 125 ASA, an excellent color print film for the amateur that produces crisp, fine-grained enlargements.

The "Amateur Photographer" plan will save you a lot of money, but it is a risky plan. You may be disappointed in the proofs when they come back from the photo lab, and there is no way to go back and take the photos again. We have all seen Uncle Fred's snapshots: the one with Aunt Minnie's head cut off or the one where everyone had their eyes closed. You only have one wedding day and one reception; if the pictures don't turn out, it can be heartbreaking. To avoid this possibility, consider these suggestions:

Guidelines For Using Amateur Photographers

1. Ask two or more amateur photographers to take pictures. Provide film for all of them. Surely, some of the pictures will turn out.

2. Request the amateurs follow my "Tips for Amateurs" at the end of this section. I have gleaned expert advice from some of the top wedding photographers in the country.

3. Be sure to have your wedding videographed also. This will provide an added assurance that you will have your day captured on film. If none of the still pictures turn out, there is a procedure whereby you can have photographs created from a videotape. The "freeze-frame" technique is used to print each image desired. This is the procedure used in police work to create a still photo from a videotape of a criminal at work. This is not to suggest that you expect any nefarious guests at your wedding, but it is a comforting emergency option just in case none of the still photography turns out. Unfortunately, this is an expensive procedure.

4. Make up a list of "must" shots for your amateur, and provide a helper who will assemble the people for these shots. The helper should be someone who knows the family members by name. You will find at the end of this section a sample list of "must" shots suggested to me by a well-known wedding photographer. Use this list for ideas.

5. A final safeguard is to supply some of your guests with disposable cameras. Have a basketful at the door when your guests arrive. These one-time-use cameras are combination camera-and-film-in-one. A roll of twenty-seven with flash is about $14. Encourage your guests to click away; then collect the mini-cameras as the guests leave. This will not only assure you of *some* kind of still photos, but you will have interesting candid shots you wouldn't have had otherwise. By the way, Kodak now offers a "Wedding Party Pack" of 5 throwaway flash cameras for approximately $45.

On behalf of amateur photographers everywhere, I would like to give a word of praise. When my husband and I were married we hired a "professional" photographer who did not get a single picture of our wedding—his film was bad. The only memories we have of our wedding are an excellent 8mm movie taken by my husband's uncle and various snapshots taken by the guests. If it weren't for these amateurs who did such a good job, we wouldn't have any pictures at all. By the way, we have since had the delightful movie transferred to a videotape, with extra copies for our children. Hurray for the amateur!

Amateur with Rented Camera
Approximate Cost. $170

Very often an amateur photographer does not have the proper camera needed to photograph a wedding. Even though he may own a fine camera, it may not have an extended flash arm or gel cell capability, for example. In this case, just rent one from a large camera store. I checked prices all over the country and it will cost you about $50 to rent the following equipment:

> One 35mm, fully automatic camera. It must have a flash arm that is at least eight inches away from the lens. The best brands are Canon, Minolta, Nikon or Pentax.
>
> One wide-angled lens.
>
> One fully charged gel cell for power. (This eliminates the problem of replacing batteries during the day.)

Arrange for your amateur to go to the camera shop to pick up the equipment personally. This way the staff can explain the camera's features and prevent unpleasant surprises later. As an extra precaution, the amateur should take a roll of film with the camera before the wedding day, to become as familiar as possible with its features. The film can be taken to a one-hour photo lab so the prints can be analyzed in plenty of time.

Artistry Only
Approximate Cost. $350

There is a relatively unknown service offered by a very few professional photographers. The professional comes to the wedding, uses his or her own camera and film and charges only for shooting the pictures. At the end of the day the photographer turns all the film over to the bride's family who will have it processed at a later date.

The advantages of this plan are obvious: you have a professional artist experienced in wedding photography with his or her own camera and film; you are relieved of the fear that the pictures won't turn out.

The disadvantage of this plan is that you may be getting an inferior photographer. Some say that photographers who work this way do so because they aren't good enough to establish a full-service business.

On the other hand, there are many satisfied customers of this type of "Artistry Only" plan. Ask for referrals; look at the photographer's work. If you feel confident, go ahead. In my town there are two excellent photographers who will work this way.

Find a Reasonable Photographer
Approximate Cost. *$600*
_____

Photography prices vary considerably depending on the artistic reputation of the photographer. The trick is to find a wonderful photographer whose reputation hasn't caught up with his or her artistic ability—one who does excellent work, but still charges a reasonable price. You do this by asking around; check with other mothers of the bride, other brides, your neighbors and friends. Try to line one up six months before the wedding, or as soon as you have set the date.

This is the route we took with our daughter's wedding. We were fortunate to find an excellent photographer who charged us $500 for a package that included:

❧ Four hours of unlimited photography

❧ A minimum of 125 preview prints

❧ One bride's album containing thirty 8×10 prints

The purchase of the remaining preview prints, the parents' albums and all other special orders were extra. This plan worked out well for us because it gave us a chance to catch our breath after the wedding and save a little money toward our own album, which we purchased four months later.

We were very pleased with our photographer who was not only artistically qualified, but calm, organized, personable and helpful. His wife accompanied him and carefully checked off the "must" shots as they were taken. They both had pleasant personalities and were a pleasure to have present on our special day.

If you decide to go with this plan, just a word of caution: get everything in writing. When will the previews be ready? Does the price include an album? If so, what quality? Exactly how many photos will be included in the album and what size? How many hours of photography are included in the price? When will the photographer arrive? I don't mean to frighten you—I just don't want you to end up on "People's Court." You know what Judge Wapner would ask: "Did you get the agreement in writing?"

Tips for Amateur Photographers

1. When using a 35mm camera, be aware that, unless your camera features a through-the-lens viewfinder, the image you see when you snap the picture is not what will be printed in the photograph. Allow extra width for group pictures. The print may be cropped on the sides cutting off the persons on the ends unless you have plenty of "air" around the group.

2. Avoid "red-eye," the eerie glow in a photo subject's eyes caused by having the flash too close to the lens. Be sure your flash is mounted, with a simple bracket, at least eight inches away from the lens. Other ways to avoid this annoying result is to have the subjects look off to the left or right of the camera or look toward the bride or another object, such as the bride's ring or flowers. Be especially careful with children because they tend to look straight at a camera. It is also possible to reduce "red-eye" by using a camera such as the Nikon Tele Touch 300 that has a unique "double-flash" feature. This feature is very helpful to the amateur photographer. "Red-eye" is caused by the reflection of light from the pupil of the eye, but with "double-flash," the first flash causes the pupil to become smaller so that less light is reflected. The second flash goes off when the picture is actually being taken, thus reducing "red-eye." In other words, the first flash "fools" the pupil into closing, the second flash takes a picture with a natural appearance.

3. Be wary of backgrounds. Watch for peculiar shapes that may look like a branch growing out of someone's head or a statue sitting on the groom's shoulder. Try to keep backgrounds as uncluttered as possible.

4. Be aware of light conditions. If you are taking outdoor shots, do not force people to look into the sun—they will squint. Face them away from the sun. And be careful not to have the bride standing in full sun while the groom is still in shadow. Keep the light exposure uniform. When photographing indoors watch for the possibility of underexposure. The bride's white dress or the white frosting on the wedding cake are the two greatest enemies of your light meter. To "trick" your camera in these two cases, take your camera off "automatic" and focus on the bride's face, then "exposure lock" this setting. This will prevent underexposure of the subjects' faces, even when you stand back to take the picture.

5. When posing the subjects, avoid lining them up like "tin soldiers." Group them in a natural way, placing heavyset or tall people in the rear. Stairways are natural settings for group shots. Most important, count to three, instructing them to keep their eyes open on "three." The biggest problem with group pictures is that someone will blink. After you have taken the picture, *ask* if anyone blinked. They will usually be honest enough to tell you so that you can take the shot again. By the way, be sure that the bride and groom are *always* in the forefront or at the top of any picture.

Good and Bad Group Photo Placements

WRONG: For group portraits, don't line the wedding party up like tin soldiers, with all the men on one side and the women on the other. Although this is a standard placement, it's not very interesting.

RIGHT: Create visual interest by using steps to stagger the heights of the wedding party. Alternate the men and women, and seat the flower girl and ring bearer at the feet of the bride and groom.

6. Capture emotions and relationships with close-ups and candid shots. Don't be afraid to come in very tight on a shot, framing only the faces of the bride and groom, for instance. And watch for hugging, touching and meaningful looks, not only between the bride and groom, but between mother and daughter or father and son. The bride and groom will appreciate the thoughtfulness of tender close-ups and candid spontaneity.

7. Be careful in the use of the flash. Check with the clergyman ahead of time to see if a flash is allowed in church. If so, only use it when the father walks the bride up the aisle and the groom walks her back down. Otherwise, use natural light with timed exposures during the ceremony.

8. Don't accidentally use up all your film on the ceremony; save plenty for the reception. It can't hurt to have a few extra rolls of film "just in case."

9. Be sensitive to people's unattractive features. For example, if the groom's mother has a banana nose that dangles over her upper lip, don't shoot her from the side; likewise, don't take a front shot of the best man if his ears stick out like satellite dishes.

10. Being an amateur, you can avoid a lot of stress by planning to take as many pictures as possible before the ceremony begins. Even if the bride doesn't want the groom to see her before the wedding, she can still have her picture taken with her mother, maid of honor, father, grandmother, etc. The same is true of the groom. Many of the "must" shots can be gotten out of the way, relieving the pressure of having to take too many shots between the ceremony and the reception. Take every formal photo possible before the wedding; this will alleviate stress after the ceremony.

11. Be a nice guy or gal. Try to be mellow, pleasant and unobtrusive. Don't boss anyone around. Make friendly suggestions, and compliment the people you are trying to photograph. They will relax and pose much more naturally with this approach. Your overall attitude will have an effect on everyone concerned. If you are loud and frenzied, everyone around you will become that way too. A quiet, polite photographer can have a calming effect on the entire event.

You will, of course, want to make up your own unique list of "must" shots. (See the following page.) There will be special people or events you will want photographed, especially in the case of an ethnic wedding. You can copy the list that follows or make up your own personalized list for your notebook. Be sure to give a copy of the list to your photographer at least a week before the wedding.

Suggested Must Shots

Bride
Bride finishing makeup
Bride with bouquet
Bride's mother or maid of honor helping with veil
Bride with mother
Bride with father
Bride with both parents
Bride with her grandparents
Bride with the children in the wedding
Bride—full length portrait
Bride with bridesmaids
Bride with groomsmen
Bride with maid or matron of honor

Groom
Groom with his parents
Groom with his mother
Groom with his father
Groom with his grandparents
Groom with the children in the wedding
Groom with groomsmen
Groom with bridesmaids
Groom with best man

Ceremony
Bride and father walking up the aisle
Timed exposures:
    Kneeling in prayer
    Lighting unity candle
    Exchanging vows
    Kiss
Bride and groom walking down the aisle

After the Ceremony
Several shots of bride and groom
Bride and groom with both parents
Bride and groom with entire wedding party

Reception
Special decorations, food displays, etc.
Couple arriving at reception
Bride and groom's first dance

Bride dancing with her father
Groom dancing with his mother
Best man's toast
Bride and groom cutting cake
Bride and groom feeding each other cake
Close-up of rings on hands of bride and groom
Bride throwing her bouquet
Groom taking off bride's garter
Groom throwing the garter
Bride and groom with those who caught the bouquet and garter
Throwing rice or bird seed
Bride and groom waving as they get into car

The Latest Trends in Candid Photography

As I mentioned in my Introduction, candid wedding photography has become very popular, often in preference to formal shots altogether. Here are some candid ideas:

- A touching shot of the bride and her father at home

- An outdoor shot with a sunrise or sunset in the background

- A shot of the bride and groom at a nearby park, swinging on their childhood swings

- If the wedding is held on a ranch or out in the country, a shot of the bride and groom sitting on a fence with their arms around the necks of a couple horses.

- A shot of the bride's and groom's empty wedding shoes, sitting side by side.

- If it's a rainy day, a humorous shot of the bride and groom ''singing in the rain'' while dancing with an umbrella.

- If it's a winter wedding with plenty of snow on the ground, a shot of the bride and groom with their arms around a snowman which has been built ahead of time by the members of the wedding party, and decorated with a top hat and scarf in the wedding colors.

- A real tight close-up shot of the bride's and groom's faces during their first dance.

🐦 A close-up shot of the couple saying goodbye to their parents after the reception.

🐦 The couple with their arms around one of their pets that has been decked out ahead of time in the wedding colors.

Cost-Cutting Videography Plans

Videography, or videotaping, has become affordable and popular with everyone these days. At least one person in the family seems to have a decent camera for recording special events. It is not difficult to understand this new popularity. For the price of a good videotape, you can have hours of live recording, complete with voices, music, sounds and antics. There isn't anyone who doesn't enjoy watching himself "on television." It holds people's interest by the hour. The whole field of wedding videography has become fierce competition to the traditional wedding photographer.

My daughter and son-in-law had their wedding professionally videotaped as a wedding gift. Because of this person's generosity, we have some very dear and emotional moments recorded forever, complete with the sounds of our daughter's laughter, the chimes on the organ, and Dad's quavering voice as he gave his daughter away. A videotape, even one made by an amateur, will become a family treasure. I've even spoken with brides who say that if they had to choose between videotape and photographs, they would pick videotape. Photographs are works of art, but videotapes are addictive entertainment!

So, I presume you will want your wedding taped, and I can't blame you. Here are some affordable ideas:

Amateur Videographer
Approximate Cost. $10

Find a friend or relative with a quality video camera, a camera with features at least as nice as the ones described in the next plan, "Amateur with a Rented VCR Camera." If possible, view some of the videotapes made by this person. If the tapes look good and you feel comfortable asking, drop a gentle hint. Perhaps this amateur will offer to tape the whole wedding and reception as a wedding gift. But you should at least offer to pay for the videotape, which must be of the finest quality, by the way.

If you have two or three friends with cameras who offer to tape your day, take them up on it. It would be nice to have at least two cameras taping during the ceremony. One could tape from the rear and one from the front, tastefully hidden from view. This would provide close-ups of the bride and groom. You would, of course, have an additional $10 cost for each videotape used.

Under this plan you will be left with unedited tape. You will not have any of the special embellishments that the professionals can add, such as graphics or commentary, but you can hardly complain about the cost! And because it is much easier to videotape a wedding than it is to photograph it, there is less chance of serious error. A photographer must assemble and pose his subjects and there is always the possibility that someone will blink, spoiling the shot. With videotaping, however, it is no problem; there is no posing or positioning—it is a spontaneous recording of events as they happen. Just be sure to have your amateurs look over the "Tips for Amateur Videographers" at the end of this chapter.

Amateur with Rented Camera
Approximate Cost. $50

If you have a willing videographer who has no camera, rent one. The average cost to rent a quality camera is about $40. This, added to the cost of the tape, will bring your total to about $50. Rent a camera with these features:

- Portable

- Battery-operated

- Half-inch color camera with recorder

- Fully automatic with playback

- One tripod

You will also want to rent two battery packs that have been fully charged. And, as with the rented still camera, be sure to have your amateur try out the camera in advance. Every camera has its own personality and you need to be sure the one you rent doesn't have the disposition of Don Rickles.

Two Amateurs with Rented Cameras
Approximate Cost. $100

As I have already mentioned, it is better to have two cameras. If you have two willing amateurs, it will only cost you $50 more to rent two cameras instead of one. This will provide that important coverage at the front of the church during the ceremony.

There is also the safety factor: it is better to have two people videotaping than one, just in case one person misses something or has problems with the camera or film.

Find a Reasonable Videographer
Approximate Cost. $200

Prices vary so drastically that it isn't difficult to find a videographer who will make a two-hour tape, nonedited, for $200. It is true that some charge over $1,000 for this same package, but you can find it for less. Again, ask around. In our town, for example, we have a major university with a lot of hungry students, some of whom will gladly videotape a wedding for less than $200. I have seen some of their work, and it is excellent. You find out about these people by talking to other brides or by calling a university (or technical college) Telecommunications Department or Instructional Materials Center (IMC). Just be sure to get your agreement in writing!

Tips for Amateur Videographers

1. Move the camera *SLOWLY!* When panning at the reception, for example, move the camera so slowly and steadily that it seems like "overkill." Use the tripod whenever possible to avoid jerky movements and remember that even your breathing can cause a "heaving" motion in the camera.

2. Likewise, zoom in and out very *SLOWLY!* A professional videotape never has any jerky motion—everything is smooth. Try your hardest to keep all camera movements as slow and smooth as possible.

3. Get close-ups of as many people as you can. The wide-angle shot is useful to establish the setting, but the close-ups are the most appreciated. Hold the camera on each shot to a minimum count of "five"; "ten" is even better. Counting to five will seem too long to you at the time, but is just right when viewing the tape later. Just remember that you are the viewers' "eyes." Don't make them seasick with sudden, jerky movements.

4. Some of the most charming tapes use live interviews—with family, friends, the minister, best man, maid of honor, the bride and groom. These interviews will bring tears and laughter in the years to come. By the way, never ask questions such as, "Do you have anything you would like to say to the bride and groom?" or "Do you have a greeting for the bride and groom?" These are "closed" questions. Instead, ask "open-ended" questions; you might ask the mother of the bride, for example, "When did you first meet your son-in-law? What was your first impression of him?" Likewise, ask the mother of the groom about the bride: "When did you first meet her?" Ask the father of the bride: "Did the groom ask you for your daughter's hand in marriage? Where were you when this happened?" Ask the bride: "How did he propose to you? Where were you? How long had you known him?" Ask Grandma: "Did you enjoy the music? What did you think of your granddaughter as she walked down the aisle?" Ask the maid of honor: "How long have you known the bride? What did you two do for fun back when you were first friends?" Ask the best man: "How long have you known the groom? Did you play sports together? Do you have any tricks planned for later? I noticed that you decorated their car."

Interview the brothers and sisters, too. Try to get them talking about their relationships with each other and things they did together when they were growing up. Do some investigative work ahead of time; know who people are and try to have some personalized questions ready. Write your questions out so that you will have them handy at the reception.

5. Practice using the camera before the wedding. Be sure that it is working properly and try using the "smooth and slow" approach.

6. Only tape on "SP," (the two-hour speed). This will give you a much better quality picture. Keep an extra videotape on hand in case you need it.

7. Try to be as inconspicuous as possible; nothing is more obnoxious than a videographer who comes on strong and attracts attention with his "party personality." Keep it low-key!

Thanks for the Memories

The day after our daughter's wedding we sat and watched the videotape; how glad I was to have the memories recorded in such a meaningful way. I watched myself on the tape as I teased my daughter in the dressing room before the wedding. As I slipped a wedding slipper onto her foot, I asked her if it fit. She said, "Yes, of course." I said, "Oh, good. Since the shoe fits, you *must* be Cinderella!" I was desperately trying to lighten things up. She was getting nervous and, although I was trying not to show it, my stomach was fluttering, too. The feeling of that moment, along with all the others, will be there to recall for a lifetime.

When the photographer's preview prints were finally ready, we reveled in the joy of selecting favorites for our albums. I spent many quiet moments with a cup of tea beside me and a kitty in my lap, savoring and reliving the precious memories of that day. You will want to capture your memories, too, so try for as many as you can—they are the perfect cure for those post-wedding blues!

10

Potpourri

(Keeping Costs Down on All Those Little Extras)

The dictionary calls "potpourri" a "miscellaneous collection," and that is exactly what I have for you in this chapter. These are the extra expenses that don't seem to fall into any of the other categories, but can really hit you unexpectedly if you aren't ready for them! Many of these "annoying pests" appear right near the end, when you think you've overcome the worst! It is just like running a race, only to discover that you can't get to the finish line without passing through a swarm of angry yellow jackets. But, have no fear, this chapter will prepare you for this encounter!

I have divided these expenses into two categories: those you will probably have to face, and those you can probably do without. When we figure your budget in the next chapter, I will always be referring to the first category. Record these expenses in your notebook under "Incidentals."

Extra Expenses You'll Probably Have to Face

Rental of Ceremony and Reception Sites
Approximate Cost. . . . . $0 to $500

Before we consider the costs of ceremony and reception sites, you should be aware of these general, common-sense considerations:

- ❦ When setting your wedding date, avoid May to October if at all possible (the priciest time of year for weddings).

- ❦ Schedule your wedding for Friday or Sunday, both of which cost far less than Saturday, especially Saturday night.

- ❦ Consider an alfresco (outdoor) wedding and reception, avoiding the cost of a hall or banquet room altogether.

❧ The most desirable, yet afforadable, sites are booked at least a year in advance, so make this one of your first decisions.

When it comes to the costs of the sites themselves, let me say that I'm well aware of the exorbitant rental fees being charged around the country, and I know many of your friends are paying these fees without a thought. Some of these pricier choices include:

❧ Country clubs

❧ Resorts

❧ Hotel ballrooms

❧ Restaurants

❧ Country inns

Not only are most of these facilities quite expensive to rent, but they also require you to order your reception food of their menu, at their prices, hire their waiters and bartenders, purchase their champagne, order your wedding cake from their bakery, pay their staff to cut and serve it and also hire the rest of their employees, as well, including coat attendants, parking valets, coordinators and florists. As you can imagine, once you've totaled all these expenses, the facility rental fee is the least of your worries.

So, what is the answer? The answer is to rent a site that is not only affordable, but gives *you* control: to provide your own home-cooked food or hire your own caterer; purchase your own champagne from Price Club by the case; allow your aunt to bake your wedding cake and let your friends cut and serve it, if that is what you choose to do. Fortunately, the most affordable wedding sites are usually those that give you this control, including these choices:

❧ *Your Own Church or Synagogue*
As far as your ceremony is concerned, your own church or synagogue is probably available to you at very little cost; that is, if you choose to have a formal ceremony in a place of worship. By the way, according to a recent poll taken by *Bride's* magazine, 87 percent of all formal weddings take place in a church, synagogue or chapel. The average cost is $200 if you are a member, if not, it's $600. Then, if you're lucky, there may also be a social hall that can be used for your reception.

❧ *Historical Sites*
Historical buildings, such as nineteenth-century libraries or

schoolhouses, provide a setting which will make your wedding unique and special. (Call your local Historical Society for suggestions.)

❦ City, County or State Facilities
Local and state governments offer some surprising choices, such as senior centers, parks, rose gardens, museums of natural history, library or courthouse grounds, marinas, clubhouses, and university or college facilities. The book *Bridges of Madison County* spurred a trend of weddings on bridges. And in California, one wedding took place in the shadow of a giant steam locomotive in the California State Railroad Museum in Sacramento; another at the sumptuous Japanese Pavilion and Gardens at Micke Grove Park near Stockton; and still another at the boat house at Oak Grove Regional Park, where the total rental fee was a mere $50 for six hours, plus gate fees.

❦ Sites Available Through the Chamber of Commerce
Your local Chamber of Commerce may have a list of sites, some of which are quite affordable, such as private mansions, art galleries, Elks halls, private wedding chapels, privately-owned gardens, ranches or farms, yachts, botanical gardens, clubhouses belonging to gated and retirement communities, and private campgrounds. Also check the yellow pages and ask around.

❦ National Parks
The federal government allows outdoor weddings to be performed in its national parks, as well. Yosemite Park in California, for example, only requires a permit of $25, which you can obtain from the Chief Ranger. The purpose of the permit, according to their public information officer, is to "keep track of where people get married and to be sure no two weddings are scheduled for the same time and place."

❦ Other Interesting Public and Private Sites
Wedding ceremonies are also being held in corporate conference rooms, private homes and gardens, hilltops, meadows, on golf course putting greens, at the seashore, on docked ferries, at the top of ski slopes, in lobbies of commercial buildings and alongside mountain streams. Look for the book entitled *Places: A Directory of Public Places for Private Events and Private Places for Public Functions*, published by Tenth House Enterprises, New York City. This fascinating book lists a variety of wedding and reception sites throughout the country, including such places as the Discovery Cove Building

at the New York Aquarium which throws in a free sea lion and walrus show with each wedding.

Invitations
Approximate Cost. . . . .$.45 × 175 = $78.75

You can pay from $1.20 to $2.45 per invitation, but this low price of only $.45 includes an inner and outer envelope, the invitation, and tissue inserts. In order to get the cost down this far, you must purchase these sets from a paper supply store. They will come blank—without any printing on them. Then, you must take them to a quick-print shop, such as PIP, who will print them at the cost of $17.70 per one hundred sets. Bring them a good laser-printed copy of your wording or a copy prepared by a calligrapher and you won't be charged the additional typesetting fee.

There are also discount printers who can provide invitations at this low cost, sometimes by mail order. Good sources for these mail-order houses are the advertisements in bridal magazines; most offer a free catalog with prices up to 50 percent off retail. Another source of inexpensive invitations is your local Hallmark store when they are having a "package special," such as this one, advertised recently in our local newspaper: "$69.95 includes 100 invitations, 100 napkins, one garter, one wedding album, two toasting glasses and one cake server."

Thank-You Notes
Approximate Cost. . . . . $.25 × 100 gifts = $25

The etiquette books say that thank-you notes only need to be plain white and, preferably, written with a fine-point black pen. The notes do not need to be engraved with initials. Therefore, buy them in bulk from the paper supply house and save that big expense.

Postage
Approximate Cost. . . $.32 × 175 invitations = $56.00

We have to pay Uncle Sam or he won't deliver our mail, but there are two ways to cut this cost: hand-deliver as many as possible or eliminate the RSVP card and envelope, which will cut your postage cost in half.

Blood Test for Bride
Approximate Cost. $40

This charge varies slightly from state to state. It can be as low as $10 through county health services or a student's health service on a college campus. Some states don't even require a blood test. The groom pays for his own test.

Mail-order Invitations

Pamela
and
Jay

Mr. and Mrs. Morris Samuelsen
and
Mr. Howard Peyton
request the honour of your presence
as their children
Pamela Jean
and
Jay Joel
share the Sacrament of Matrimony
A Wedding Mass will celebrate this union
Saturday, the twentieth of October
Nineteen hundred and ninety
at ten o'clock in the morning
St. Bonaventure Catholic Church
16400 Springdale Street
Huntington Beach, California

Rexcraft No. 2258

Mr. and Mrs. Lester Vincent Doyle
request the honour of your presence
at the marriage of their daughter
Paige Allison
to
Mr. Frederick Brian Gregory
Saturday, the seventh of April
Nineteen hundred and ninety
at seven o'clock in the evening
Church of the Savior
4244 Genessee Boulevard
Aurora, Colorado

Sugar 'n Spice No. 262

At least ten companies offer a variety of beautiful yet inexpensive wedding invitations by mail order. Most have toll-free numbers and will send free catalogs and samples. Check recent issues of bridal magazines for advertisements.

Marriage License

Approximate Cost. *$28*

This varies from state to state—most are a little lower, and California is a little higher.

Favors

Approximate Cost. . . . .*$.40 × 150 = $60.00*

After much research, I came up with ten inexpensive favors that you can make yourself. You generally only give favors to female guests so you will need 150 for a wedding of 300 guests. Most of the supplies listed below can be purchased at a floral supply house. The favors range in price from $.11 to $1.03 each. Here they are:

Blue Net With Almonds

Tie blue tulle (thin netting) around two or three Jordan almonds, securing with narrow ribbon. As you tie the bow, include a small pearl heart.

Bag of 400 Jordan almonds	$ 9.00
One roll tulle (cut 6″ × 6″)	12.75
150 small pearl hearts	12.10
One roll narrow ribbon (100 yards)	4.50
Total	$38.35

(This will make 150 favors @ $.26 each)

Almond Favors With Dove

Wrap three almonds with the netting rounds. Wire one dove around the top and tie with double ribbons.

Bag of 400 Jordan almonds	$ 9.00
Three bags netting rounds	27.75
One bag doves on wire	10.45
Two rolls ribbon	9.25
Total	$56.45

(This will make 144 favors @ $.39 each)

Champagne Glasses With Almonds

Fill champagne glass with two or three almonds and cover top with tulle, bringing it down to the stem of the glass. Secure with ribbon and a tiny silk flower.

150 small plastic champagne glasses	$25.50
Bag of 400 Jordan almonds	9.00
One roll tulle	4.50
One roll (100 yards) + 10 yards ribbon	13.50
Four stems silk flowers	6.00
Total	$58.50

(This will make 150 favors @ $.39 each)

Netted Soaps

Purchase decorative soaps at $.20 each. Tie them up with tulle and ribbon with double-bows.

150 soaps	$30.00
One roll (100 yards) + 10 yards ribbon	13.50
One roll tulle	4.50
Total	$48.00

(This will make 150 favors @ $.32 each)

Netted Potpourri

Buy sacks of herbs and spices and enclose small portions in tulle netting. Tie with ribbon and one flower.

Two pounds potpourri	$26.00
One roll tulle	4.50
One roll narrow ribbon (100 yards)	4.50
Four stems silk flowers	6.00
Total	$41.00

(This will make 150 favors @ $.27 each)

Netted Bird Seed

Throwing rice has passed out of fashion; it evidently can make birds very sick because they eat too much and it swells in their stomachs. So, it has become popular to throw bird seed instead. Wrap golf-ball-size portions of seed in net; tie with ribbon and a tiny silk flower.

Twenty-four pounds bird seed	$15.00
One roll tulle	4.50

One roll narrow ribbon	4.50
Four stems silk flowers	6.00
Total	$30.00

(This will make 150 favors @ $.20 each)

The guests, of course, aren't required to untie the favors and toss the bird seed at the bride and groom—they may take them home if they wish.

Decorated Candles

Decorate the "handle" or bottom of an 8-inch candle with tufted netting and tiny silk flowers. At the end of the reception give one to each guest to light and use to form a "going-away" path for the bride and groom; this idea only works, of course, for an evening wedding.

Two rolls tulle netting	$15.00
150 8-inch candles	78.00
Four stems silk flowers (approximately forty tiny blooms to tie or glue to the tulle base)	6.00
Total	$99.00

(This will make 150 favors @ $.66 each)

Decorated Seed Packets With Notes Attached

Give each guest a decorated packet of seeds with a personalized note attached which reads something like this: "As these seeds bloom into flowers, may they remind you of how much we love you." Cut each sheet of paper lengthwise into three, then into five across for fifteen notes per sheet. Copy centers sell individual sheets of parchment and other decorative paper for about $.10 each.

150 packets of seeds	$58.50
10 sheets of 8½″ × 14″ parchment paper	5.00
Total	$63.50

(This will make 150 favors @ $.42 each)

Polaroid Photo Favors

As each single guest or couple arrives at the reception, take their picture using a Polaroid camera; then, attach each photo to a designated tree at the reception, along with a loving note from the bride and groom thanking the guests for sharing the day, etc. As the guests leave, ask them to search the tree for their photos which they may keep as favors.

Polaroid film (when purchased in a 3-pack from a discount store, approximately $1.00 per photo)	$150.00
10 sheets of 8½″ × 14″ parchment paper	5.00
Total	$155.00

(This will make 150 favors @ $1.03 each)

Personal Message Rolled into a Scroll

This is the idea our daughter and son-in-law used. They wrote a personal message, thanking the guests for sharing the day with them, etc. Then they had this message copied onto a "master" by a calligrapher. This was duplicated nine times onto a legal-sized sheet of plain white paper. This sheet was then used as the "master" to be copied onto 23 pieces of parchment paper. It required that much parchment cut into nine "scrolls" each, to give them 207 scrolls. (One was given to each single person or couple.) Each of the scrolls was rolled up and tied with a narrow ribbon and two small gold rings.

Twenty-three pieces of 8½″ × 14″ parchment paper	$11.50
Twenty-three copies on copy machine	2.30
Ribbon	4.50
Gold-colored rings	4.00
Total	$22.30

(This will make 207 favors @ $.11 each)

Last-Minute Alterations
Approximate Cost. ***$50***

There will be unexpected glitches in the way everything fits, from bridesmaids' dresses to the wedding gown. People sometimes lose or gain weight close to the wedding.

It will usually save you quite a bit of money if you forego the seamstress at the bridal salon and provide for your own alterations; some bridal salons charge as much as $250 to alter a wedding gown.

Guest Book and Pen
Approximate Cost. *$12*

You can purchase a fancy set for up to $35 or you can buy a plain book with "Guests" printed on the cover, the type intended to be used in your home. The inside pages are the same. Use a plain white ball-point pen tied with a ribbon.

Guest Book Alternatives
Parchment Scroll *$1*

Modern brides have come up with some other interestng alternatives to the standard wedding guest book, as well: one idea is to provide a long piece of off-white parchment paper that you roll into a tight scroll and then let unwind, creating a lovely document for your guests to sign. After the wedding, this scroll may be kept as a memento by framing it or re-rolling it and tying with a ribbon.

Wedding Guest Artwork. *$35*

Another trendy idea is to provide sheets of paper, along with crayons and felt-tip markers (one set per table) for the guests to write messages or draw pictures—a truly clever alternative to the traditonal guest book.

Engagement Photo With Extra-Wide Matting *$10*

Have your guests sign a wide white matting around your engagement photo, as it stands on a floor easel at eye level at the reception. (The $10 covers the cost of the matting and doesn't include the cost of the photo.)

Kneeling Bench or Cushion
Approximate Cost. *$10*

If a kneeling bench is required for your ceremony, borrow one from the church itself. If they don't have one, rent one from a florist or wedding rental store. Rental benches run from $5 to $18.

Table Skirts

Approximate Cost. . . . . *3 × $8 ea. = $24*

You will be able to borrow the table linen for the reception, but most people don't have table skirts. The disposable variety are fine and only cost $8 each.

Sheet Music for Musicians

Approximate Cost. *$10*

A church organist and the other musicians will almost always have the music you need for your wedding. However, you will probably need to buy at least one piece of music that no one seems to have. In our case, we purchased the "Wedding March" from *The Sound of Music* for the organist to play as the recessional.

Ring Bearer's Pillow

Approximate Cost. *$12*

Although you can spruce up an old Easter basket for the flower girl, the ring bearer does need a clean, white satin pillow. If you can borrow or make one, you can save the money; otherwise, watch for a sale.

Garters for the Bride

Approximate Cost. *$10*

You will need two garters: one to keep and one to toss. In our daughter's case, the one she kept was the one I wore when I was married. Sometimes these are available in sets of two for $7 or $8.

Grand total of probable miscellaneous expenses: $677.75

Ouch! That stings, doesn't it? I told you these annoying expenses are like a swarm of yellow jackets; at least you have been warned and won't be unpleasantly surprised later. These costs are usually ignored because the bride's family is so concerned about the dress, the cake, the flowers and all the other seemingly larger expenses. And because these expenses don't seem to fit into a category, they go off by themselves and multiply like rabbits in the summertime and suddenly appear in the form of huge dollar signs. Well, in the next chapter these expenses are added into the totals, so you will cross your finish line without pain.

Extra Expenses You Can Probably Do Without:

Luggage for the Honeymoon
If you don't already have enough pieces for your trip, borrow them.

Clergyman's Fee

This fee is the responsibility of the groom and will vary from $50 to $400.

Aisle Runner

Do without it! Even most White House weddings do without an aisle runner because the wedding dress photographs better against a darker color. We didn't have a runner, and the dark blue carpet really set off our daughter's dress. Also, if the aisle runner is very white, it can make an off-white wedding gown look dirty.

Going-Away Outfit

Wear something you already have. Also, it has become popular to go on the "wedding parade" in the full wedding attire and then change into very casual clothes before leaving on the honeymoon. Some brides and grooms even wear blue jeans.

Makeup Artist

"Facial artistry," as it is called, has become the fad lately. There are professionals who will come in for an hourly rate and make up the entire wedding party. Instead, have the bridesmaids make each other up, and have the maid or matron of honor assist the bride. You can get free make-over ideas beforehand by having a professional apply your makeup at a finer department store cosmetic department. The important thing to remember is to take it easy on the makeup—don't overdo it to the point where the bride doesn't even look like herself, which often happens when an amateur goes crazy.

Hair Appointments

Unless your hair is very difficult to manage, have a friend or another family member help you with it.

Manicures

In the same way, do each others' nails. They will be beautiful!

Groom's Cake

A groom's cake is very popular in the South, but often omitted at weddings elsewhere around the country. It is almost always a dark fruitcake, but it can also be dark chocolate. It can be cut up in tiny squares and placed in little white boxes with the bride and groom's initials or it can just be served on a separate table from the bride's cake for those who prefer a different flavor. If you have a loving grandma who would love to bake fruitcakes for the occasion, that would be very nice, but it certainly isn't a necessary expense.

Nursery

Some etiquette books say that a wedding is no place for small children; however, most daytime weddings I have attended seem to have plenty of them running around. That is why an attended nursery can be a delightful convenience for the parents, including the wedding party who may have small children. We provided paid nursery workers for our daughter's wedding, but it certainly is not an expected service. Our cost was $45 total for the wedding rehearsal and ceremony only. During the reception, the parents were on their own.

Bride and Groom's Engraved Champagne Glasses

Borrow the most beautiful glasses you can find; just tie each with white satin ribbon. If you decide to buy a set, they run $18 at a wedding supply store.

Cake Server

Borrow a nice silver one from a friend or relative; tie with white satin ribbon. If you decide to buy one, it will run $30.

Note: Always look for package deals, usually advertised as "Wedding Ensembles" that include several of these "extras" in one price. For example, the current JCPenney Bridal Collection catalog offers an ensemble for $70 that includes: bride's file box, two champagne goblets, one plume pen with stand, one heart-shaped satin ring bearer's pillow with lace, two garters, one wedding album, and a cake knife and server set with pearlized handles.

Programs for the Ceremony

Programs are nice to have because they identify the members of the wedding party. They also give the order of the ceremony so that the guests can follow along. You can make up a good computer master that you can copy and fold yourself for a total of about $15. Otherwise, forget them. Only about half the weddings I attend furnish them anyway.

Lighting Technician

If the church or synagogue's lighting system is complex, the church may offer their lighting person who will assist for a nominal fee. Otherwise, see if you can find a talented friend to help. In our case, the available lighting was no problem; we just turned it on and adjusted it before the service and no extra help was needed.

Calligrapher

Some brides hire a calligrapher to address all the invitations, reply envelopes, and thank-you notes. A calligrapher charges by the hour and it takes many hours to complete this task. In my daughter's case, we bought the proper type of black calligraphy pen and I did them myself. I took it nice and slow and used a few extra "loops" and "twirls." Some people thought we had them done professionally, but actually anyone with decent handwriting can do a lovely job if they have the right pen and plenty of time.

If you really have your heart set on using a calligrapher, you might check into using a marvelous new machine called an "Inscribe Calligraphy Bed" that writes in original calligraphy, using an actual calligraphy pen of your choice. Because the machine does the writing instead of a human being, the cost is quite reasonable.

Lodging for Out-of-Town Guests and/or Wedding Party

This expense is usually paid by the guests or members of the wedding party. If the bride's family feels, however, that this would be a burdensome expense, they can make other arrangements. One suggestion is to ask friends and other family members to "put them up." Another idea is to rent a self-contained recreational vehicle that can be parked in your driveway at a cost of about $60 per day. The one I saw for this price was twenty-four feet long and slept eight people.

Linen Tablecloths, Punch Bowls, Serving Plates, etc.

If the reception is held in a social hall connected to the church or synagogue, everything you need will be available in the rental fee for the site. If you must provide anything yourself, borrow like crazy. There are white linen tablecloths sitting in drawers all over town, as well as punch bowls of all sizes and lovely serving platters and bowls. After a couple of phone calls, you will have everything you need and more.

Last-Minute Pressing of Bridesmaids' Dresses or Other Attire

We brought three dresses to the dry cleaners at the last minute to have them "touched up." One had been in a suitcase and the other two had never been pressed out when purchased. We paid $6 to have one pressed and $9 each for two bridesmaids' dresses. This was more for convenience than anything. To save these costs, just keep your ironing board up, use a good press cloth, and do it yourself.

11

Tips for Your Groom

(Money-Saving Ideas for the Man in Your Life)

I assume your fiancée has handed this book over to you so you can save some money, too. Am I right? Because over 70 percent of brides and grooms are paying for the entire wedding themselves, chances are that your savings are quickly being depleted. Even if you aren't sharing in the cost of the wedding itself, you are undoubtedly being saddled with these incidental expenses already discussed in previous chapters:

    ❦ Your share of the florist's bill

    ❦ The clergyman's fee

    ❦ Your blood test and the marriage license

    ❦ The rental or purchase of your wedding attire

In addition to these expected expenses, you have five more that are yours exclusively:

    ❦ Bride's Engagement Ring

    ❦ Wedding Bands

    ❦ The Getaway Vehicle

    ❦ A Gift For Your Bride

    ❦ The Honeymoon

I have some brilliant ideas for you for each of these items—not all of which are my brain children for, I must admit, I have interviewed hundreds of grooms who have agreed to share their money-saving ideas with you.

First of all, let's talk about wedding jewelry and the best ways to have high quality on a small budget.

Bride's Engagement Ring

I don't know if you've already shopped for her ring, but if you've been window-shopping in retail jewelry store windows, you're probably still pale from the sticker-shock! First of all, the worst place to go shopping is your retail jewelry store, unless they're having a whopping-good sale. Here are some smart alternatives:

Family Heirloom Ring
No cost $0

If you're lucky, there may be a lovely heirloom ring rattling around a dresser drawer somewhere in your family; it may be an antique setting passed down from your great-grandmother, or an exquisite dinner ring sitting in a safety-deposit box, leftover from your great-aunt's estate. Give this idea some serious thought because an heirloom ring may be the most poignant, touching gift you can give her.

Set an Existing Diamond
Approximate Cost. . . . . $75–$125

If you have been given an heirloom ring, but the setting is inappropriate, you can have the existing diamond(s) lifted out of the antique ring and placed in a new setting. In one case, a man was given his grandfather's Masonic ring which had a black onyx base on top of a heavy gold band with a large center diamond; he took the ring to the jeweler's and had the gold in the band melted down into a modern Tiffany setting and the single diamond lifted and used to create a stunning solitaire engagement ring.

There are other sources of used diamonds, as well, such as estate sales, pawn shops and classified ads. However, these are risky places to shop for a diamond and I don't recommend them because it is usually impossible to verify the diamond's authenticity before making the purchase; if you have a knowledgeable friend who will accompany you, or if you are allowed to bring the diamond or piece of jewelry to a professional appraiser before committing yourself, this may be a possibility.

Set a Temporary Synthetic Diamond
Approximate cost. $100

Here is an idea that is gaining popularity, but it is only a possibility if your bride goes along with the idea. For the time being, purchase a synthetic diamond which is the same size as the authentic diamond you plan to replace it with at a later date. Surprisingly, this clever idea was revealed to me in confidence by several retail jewelers who told me how popular this trick has become, and every one of them admitted that, unless someone has a trained eye, a good quality synthetic diamond looks enough like the real thing to "fool the girls at the office," at least until the groom can afford to replace it with the genuine article when his finances straighten out after the honeymoon.

If you decide to pursue this idea, however, be sure your bride approves of this clandestine plan, and, most important: Don't share this beautifully devious news with anyone! It will be your own little secret—just between you and your bride. Then, on a later date—perhaps as a Christmas or birthday gift, or on your first anniversary—you will have the joy of presenting her with the diamond of her choice.

Give an Engagement Ring with a Birthstone Instead of a Diamond

Approximate Cost. . . . . **$100–$500**

An engagement ring doesn't have to be set with a diamond to be "official"; there are many other stones that are quite beautiful, as well, including aquamarine, pearl, opal and amethyst.

Buy It Wholesale for 50 Percent Off Retail Price

By shopping around you can find ways to purchase a new ring of your choice without having to pay full retail price. One of the best sources is your wholesale diamond broker, often accessible only when accompanied by someone with a seller's resale permit, although many are also available to the public. The good news is when you purchase a diamond ring from one of these brokers, you will usually save at least 50 percent off retail. The bad news is that you will have to pay cash on the spot.

Other ways to save 50 percent off retail is to purchase through a discount catalog store, such as Best, through JCPenney Bridal Collection or a bridal gift registry catalog, or though a retailer who may be having a special limited-time 50 percent off retail sale, often during the two week period precdeding Valentine's Day.

Just remember that by shopping around you can find a diamond your fiancée will love at a discount of 50 percent, or more, off the suggested retail price.

Warning: Become Fluent in the "Four Cs"

Regardless of where youplan to shop for your bride's diamond, you need to be educated in the Four Cs:

❦ *Clarity*

Clarity is ranked on a scale from *F1* (flawless) to *F13* (imperfect); the differences in clarity are said to be difficult to discern with the naked eye. An *F1* diamond can run from $1,000 to $5,000 more than a comparable diamond with an *F13* ranking.

❦ *Color*

Color refers to the color of the diamond itself, which ranges from *D* (colorless) to *Y* (yellow). This quality is more discernible to the naked eye, but usually only when diamonds are compared side by side in strong sunlight. The price differences between a *D* and a *Y* ranking are similar to those for clarity; a *D* being the higher priced.

❧ *Carat*

Carat indicates the weight of the diamond; a one carat diamond, for example, weighs twice as much and is twice the size of a half carat diamond. The carat weight is obviously the most discernible quality to the naked eye. The average carat weight of an engagement ring diamond in the United States today, by the way, is .75; this is according to a recent survey published in *USA Today.*

❧ *Cut*

The cut of the diamond refers to its shape and number of facets; the general shape of the diamond is easy to see, but the number of facets are not as obvious. The more facets, the more brilliance as you turn the diamond back and forth under a strong light.

My own little personal survey, by the way, shows that most women prefer a larger diamond that has a few "invisible" flaws over a smaller one that is closer to perfect.

When you go shopping for a diamond, a one-carat, colorless, flawless Marquise cut will probably be the first you will be shown by the jeweler, who hopes to sell you one of his more expensive pieces. Be prepared to be hit with the "two-months' salary" rule, which is a rule of thumb, conveniently calculated by jewelers and diamond merchants who want you to spend two months' of your salary on the ring. Remember that this is *their* idea, not yours, and you should spend no more than is comfortable for you. Don't forget that you can always add a more expensive setting or an extra diamond or two some day when your income is higher and you don't have so many other wedding and honeymoon expenses to pay for all at once.

Wedding Bands

Create Wedding Bands from Used Gold
Approximate cost . . . . **$100–$125**

Used gold is much easier to round up than a used diamond, and many couples are having their wedding bands poured from old, removed gold fillings or bridgework or from existing gold jewelry, whether antique or not. One groom I know brought a gold bridge and a couple gold caps to his jeweler, along with an old gold ring that had been in his family, hoping the total ounces would be enough to create a "chunky" wedding band for himself. The result was that the dental gold alone was more than enough for a large band that would have retailed for over $800; his total cost, however, was only $125. The family ring contained enough gold to pour a wedding band for his bride, as well, for an additional cost of only $100. So, you see? If you have any gold dental work replaced, be sure to take it home with you, and do some "constructive snooping" among your family members to see if anyone has an old gold chain in need of repair, a bracelet, ring or pin which could be melted down and poured into the mold of your choice. Brilliant idea!

Wedding Bands at 50 Percent Off Retail Price
Approximate cost . . . . *$75–$125*

Shop for your bands from the same discount sources mentioned earlier: wholesale jewelry brokers; discount catalog stores or JCPenney's bridal catalog; or, through a retail jewelry store that is having a sale.

The Getaway Vehicle

It is a trend these days to hire one limousine to serve triple-duty:

1. Transporting the wedding party to the ceremony site

2. Transporting the bride and groom from the ceremony to the reception

3. As a getaway vehicle for the bride and groom

This is fine and good except that limousines don't come cheap, averaging approximately $80 per hour, plus tips. Frankly, they have become just a little boring, wouldn't you say? After all, you can't even see through the darkened glass, so they're no fun at all for the guests!

Here are some interesting, affordable alternatives that you might want to consider, depending on where you live and who you know:

❧ *Borrow or Rent a Cadillac or Lincoln Town Car*
Know any affluent friends or relatives who might loan you their luxury vehicle for the day? Or, do as one couple did—rent a Town Car for $40.00 for twenty-four hours, which certainly beats the cost of a limo!

❧ *Any Convertible*
Tie on the balloons and streamers and sit on top of the back seat as you leave the reception. A convertible works especially well because there's plenty of room for the bride's gown and veil.

❧ *A Decorated Jeep*
One couple I know decorated an old rusty Jeep, wrapping it in white crepe paper and decorating it with paper flowers, streamers and balloons and then "skirting" it with disposable, white plastic

ruffled table skirting. The wedding party had fun decorating it and when they were finished they had an elegant "float" for showing off the bride and groom on the ride from the reception to the airport.

❦ A Decorated Pickup Truck

The same idea works for a pickup truck by "skirting" and "ballooning" the bed where the bride and groom sit on decorated lawn chairs for the wedding parade through town.

❦ Hay Wagon

How about an old-fashioned hay ride? In one case the entire wedding party piled aboard the hay bales, escorted the bride and groom to the airport and then continued on their way, not wanting the party to end. It's great if you have a farmer or rancher in the family, otherwise, any flat bed truck or trailer will do. If you have to rent, the rental plus the bales of hay will run about $200.00.

❦ A Snowmobile or Horse-Drawn Sleigh

If you're marrying in the winter and there's plenty of snow on the ground, you might want to consider one of these fun alternatives. A horse and sleigh rig will rent for $100 to $500 for the day.

❦ A Classic or Antique Car

If you know anyone who has a cute old car, whether a Model T or '55 Chevy, ask if you can borrow or rent it for the wedding. A good source is your local classic car club where the members are so "into" their vehicles you may even find one who will offer to serve as your driver, just for a chance to personally show off his toy.

❦ Up, Up and Away

You may be one of those lucky people who just happens to know a hot air balloonist or someone who has access to a helicopter. Wouldn't that make a dramatic statement as you "lift off"?

❦ Novelty Getaways

You can really wow them by galloping off on horseback (be sure to braid the horses' tails and manes with white satin ribbons!), chugging away in a little red tractor, peddling off on a decorated bicycle-built-for-two, or, how about a little yellow school bus?

The important thing is to look for novel, affordable opportunities. You might even come up with an idea that won't cost you a penny, except for the fuel. And here's an extra tip: if your vehicle requires a driver, rent him his own top hat!

A Gift For Your Bride

The bride and groom usually talk over their gift-giving ideas so that they are on the same wavelength when it comes to buying gifts for each other and, in fact, many couples decide to forego these gifts and put their money toward the wedding or their honeymoon. On the other hand, it's very special to give your bride a personal gift, something she will treasure always—a gift from her husband on her wedding day! And it's usually a good idea for this gift to be something lasting, something your bride can touch, hold or wear throughout her married life.

Here are some affordable, yet meaningful, choices:

Cultured Pearl Necklace or Earrings
> *Approximate cost. . . . . $40–$160*

Depending on whether you choose a single pearl on a gold chain, a strand of pearls or a pair of pearl earrings, your gift will be quite affordable if you shop the discount market, as I have already described. Best Company, for example, recently offered a 23-inch string of cultured pearls for only $160 or cultured pearl earrings for $110. Note: there are simulated pearls and cultured pearls, and it is the latter which is considered suitable as a wedding gift.

Diamond Drop Necklace or Earrings
> *Approximate cost. . . . . $130–$400*

Diamonds are obviously more expensive than pearls, but again, if you shop the discount market, you will find a stunning gift within this price range.

14K Gold Heart Pendant or Locket
> *Approximate cost. . . . . Under $100*

You can find a beautifully engraved heart-shaped pendant or locket on a gold chain for less than $100, again by shopping the discount market.

Precious Moments Figurine
> *Approximate cost. . . . . $50–$70*

Here is a sweet, poignant gift idea, especially if your bride happens to be a fan of Precious Moments. For about $70 you can purchase one of these figurines, entitled "I Give You My Love Forever True," a bride and groom with flowers at their feet that stands about six and a half inches high. Another, entitled "Sealed With a Kiss," sells for about $60; it is a bisque figurine of a bride and groom kissing over the mailbox of their new home and stands about five and a half inches high. All Precious Moments figurines are collectibles that should appreciate in value every year; they can be purchased at most gift shops, Hallmark stores and through various catalogs, including JCPenney's Bridal Gift Registry catalog.

Music Box
> Approximate cost . . . . *$30–$60*

If you're the sentimental type and you really want to wow your bride with a "warm, fuzzy" gift, how about a music box? Most women love music boxes. These lovely, yet affordable, gifts can be purchased at Hallmark stores, department stores, gift shops, The San Francisco Music Box Company (often found in shopping malls), or through a discount catalog store. One of my favorite music boxes has an open porcelain book with a love poem written on one page, two love doves perched on the other, and plays the song "Wind Beneath My Wings."

Book of Love Poems
> Approximate cost . . . . *$6–$20*

Don't let the frugality of this gift fool you—any bride would love to receive a book of love poems from her groom, especially if he writes something endearing on the dedication page. A popular choice is a book by Elizabeth Barrett Browning entitled *Sonnets from the Portuguese.* Or, if you're a poet, write her something truly original to express your love for her and your feelings about your wedding day. For only six dollars you can purchase a "blank book," a beautifully bound book that has empty pages, all ready and waiting for your original verse (or, you can cheat a little and steal some ideas from some of those mushy love cards at Hallmark!).

The Honeymoon

Ah, finally we come to our biggest expense of all—the honeymoon! If you're like most grooms-to-be, you're probably wondering how there will ever be enough money left over for that wonderfully romantic honeymoon you have in mind. Well, I sympathize with you, but take a big breath and read on, for there *is* hope—I guarantee it!

I have written an entire book on this subject entitled *How to Have a Fabulous, Romantic Honeymoon on a Budget,* and you may wish to pick up a copy; however, here are some of the best ideas my book has to offer, along with a couple very novel money-saving honeymoon ideas I picked up in my course as editor and columnist for *Honeymoon Magazine.*

According to a recent *Bride's Magazine* poll, the average cost of a honeymoon is $3,200. Assuming your bank account is down to $1,500, or $1,000, or even less, here are your best honeymoon buys, categorized by price range.

Free Honeymoons

A free honeymoon! Is there such a thing! You bet there is, and here's how you have it:

Honeymoon Gift Registry

Establish a gift registry at your favorite travel agency, in the same way you would establish a registry at a department store or gift shop. Spread the word, cross your fingers, and hope that enough comes in to pay for your *entire* honeymoon! If your only registry is through a travel agency, you're more likely to have enough.

Hideaway Honeymoon at Home

This is one of the brilliant ideas I discovered as editor of *Honeymoon Magazine*. I had no idea so many couples were doing this! Here's the drill:

1. Tell everyone you're flying to the Bahamas (or somewhere) for your honeymoon.

2. Don't tell *anyone* you're actually honeymooning in your own home or apartment—not *even* your parents or best man!

3. A few days before the wedding, stock your "secret honeymoon nest" with goodies: prepared foods from the deli; plenty of things to drink including, of course, champagne; paper plates, cups, plastic champagne glasses; candles (lots and lots of candles!); romantic CDs and tapes; bubble bath; massage oil; an ample supply of sheets and towels; fresh strawberries; several boxes of chocolates; your favorite cologne and perfume; and a couple dozen movies on video (not that you'll really watch them all, of course).

4. Bring packed suitcases with you to the reception that can be placed (in full view of your guests) in the trunk of your getaway vehicle to convince everyone you're really flying off somewhere!

5. Be sure you aren't followed home after the reception. If necessary, head for the airport and stay on that route until you've ditched the last of the wedding party who may be following you.

6. Once you're home, hide your car in the garage, unplug the telephone and don't answer the door—no matter what!

Isn't this a deliciously devious idea? Of course, in a year or so you'll be able to afford that exotic honeymoon you originally had in mind, and you'll appreciate it all the more by then.

Honeymoons Less Than $600

❦ Borrow or Rent an RV or a Houseboat

What could be more romantic than the sound of raindrops pinging against the metal roof of your RV or houseboat as you cuddle in a sleeping bag made for two, or the smell of bacon frying over an open campfire alongside a secluded lake in a national park, or a walk in the moonlight along a deserted beach? Give it some thought—you may even have a friend or relative who would loan you a cozy unit, cutting your cost even further.

❧ A Long-Weekend Honeymoon

Stay at picturesque, but affordable, spots in your home state that include at least one meal in the price, such as a bed-and-breakfast; then go everywhere and do everything that's ''fun but cheap'': sight-seeing and people-watching; attending free festivals; poking around a flea market; free-loading dinner off a ''happy hour buffet'' for the price of a couple of drinks; lunching with a picnic basket full of romantic goodies at the beach or a scenic overlook. When a couple is in love, it's amazing how fun and wonderful and romantic everything seems to be, because, as we all know, it's *who you're with* that really counts!

Honeymoons Less Than $1,000

Your best chance to have a really fabulous time on your honeymoon in this price range is to purchase a *package deal*; by this I mean a honeymoon that is all-inclusive, with no mysterious hidden or unexpected costs. Believe it or not, there are actually quite a few honeymoons that fit this category:

❧ Take a Short Cruise

Depending on where you live and how easy it is for you to get to the point of embarkation, there are honeymoon cruises available for about $500 per person, all-inclusive. Several embark from Florida ports (so you will have to pay to get to Florida) including one with Sunday departures on the Dolphin Sea Breeze with stops at Nassau, San Juan, St. John and St. Thomas, and another takes a more southerly route to Playa del Carmen, Cozumel, Montego Bay and Grand Caymen. These honeymoon cruises usually include a honeymoon cocktail party, champagne, fruit in your room and a surprise gift. Other cruises leave out of Los Angeles and visit Catalina Island, Ensenada, Cabo San Lucas, or various romantic ports along the west coast of mainland Mexico. Call one of the discount cruise companies to get the best rates, such as The Cruise Line, Inc. at (800) 777-0707.

❧ Escape to the Poconos!

The Pocono Honeymoon Resorts, located in the Pocono Mountains of Pennsylvania, absolutely drip with sensuality, with their deep, heart-shaped Whirlpool tubs, private swimming pools, velvet-draped canopied beds, candlelit dinners, free entertainment and recreational opportunities. It's no wonder their all-inclusive packages are such honeymoon favorites. Call 1-800-POCONOS for free brochures.

✾ *Rent a Private Residence, Cabin or Condo*

Contact the Visitor's Bureau at your honeymoon destination and ask for a list of rental agencies who offer private rentals. Even Lake Tahoe, which is a picture perfect Honeymoon setting, has offerings starting at about $400 per week. Then, of course, you will need to do a little cooking, or bring in deli or take-out foods, which should leave money left over for a couple of splurges.

✾ *Nightlife-Wilderness Combo*

You can enjoy the nightlife of Las Vegas, which is actually quite affordable if you take advantage of the free entertainment, all-you-can-eat buffets and nearby "nature escapes" to the Black Canyon. For example, if you stay at The Mirage, (800) 627-6667, you can enjoy four nights' stay with enough money left over for a float down the Colorado River with the Black Canyon River Raft Tours, (800) 696-RAFT. If you live in the East, give the Grand Casino in Gulfport, Mississippi a call at (800) 354-2450 where $1,000 will cover four nights, five days, all your meals and the resort's many amenities, including their own swimming beach on the gulf.

✾ *Walt Disney World "Honeymoon Escape"*

As this book goes to press, Walt Disney World in Orlando, Florida is offering a honeymoon package priced at $849 per couple that includes four nights, five days at their hotel; use of their transportation system; daily admissions to all their attractions, including the Magic Kingdom, Epcot and the MGM Studios; a "romance basket"; use of bicycles, canoes, sailboats, pedal boats; and more. Call them at (407) 934-7639.

Honeymoons Less Than $1,500

✾ *Take a Longer Cruise*

Call The Cruise Line, Inc. at the number mentioned earlier, or any discount cruise company of your choice, for longer honeymoon cruises. If you can afford $1,500 for your honeymoon, there are several romantic cruises available at about $750 per person.

✾ *Fly or Drive to Mexico or Canada*

Our neighbors to the north and south offer some very affordable stays, depending on how close you live to one of their borders.

Empire Tours, Suntrips, Delta Dream Vacations and American Airlines Fly A'Away Vacations offer some of the best packages to cities in Mexico, including Cancun, Puerto Vallarta, Mazatlan, Los Cabos, Mexico City and Guadalajara.

Canada is an easy destination if you live anywere near their border. If you're in the northwest, visit Vancouver, Victoria and the San Juan Islands or cross over to Prince Albert in Saskatchewan and visit the Prince Albert National Park; or visit Winnipeg in Manitoba which offers many scenic walking tours and people-watching opportunities; or, the city of Quebec will give you the feeling of being in old Paris where you can stay quite reasonably at Le Chateau de Pierre, a converted mansion located in Old Quebec Uppertown; if you live in the northeast, how about a little ferry boat ride up to Cavendish and Prince Edward Island, nick-named the Playground Province, where you can enjoy water sports galore?

❦ An Adventure Honeymoon

You can stay well within the $1,500 range by planning a sporting or adventure honeymoon. You may want to charter a boat for a deep-sea-fishing trip, or sign up for a golfer's package or reserve a week at a dude ranch or guest ranch. (Word of caution: Look for one that is "adults-only.") If the fishing idea sounds good, go to your local magazine stand and purchase several of the fishing magazines, including *Sport Fishing, Field and Stream* or *Outdoor Life*, where you will find ads for various package trips. If you're a golfer, of course, look for ads in *Golf* or *Golf Digest*, and if the dude ranch idea is appealing, go to your library or purchase Gene Gilgore's book entitled *Ranch Vacations*.

The important thing to remember is that the success of your honeymoon doesn't depend on how much you spend, but the fact that you can be together, uninterrupted, after the stress and hoopla of the wedding plans and your wedding day itself. Any setting is a romantic setting, after all, when you only have eyes for each other and are relishing your new roles as husband and wife.

Cost-Cutting Tips While You're on Your Honeymoon

Meanwhile, no matter where you spend your honeymoon, here are some general common-sense cost-cutting tips:

❦ Be sure to pack plenty of film, toothpaste, shampoo and suntan lotion, the four things most likely to need replacing at your honeymoon site where they will cost more than at your hometown discount drug store.

🐦 Don't even think of touching your hotel room's mini-bar.

🐦 Don't phone home—too expensive, especially if from your hotel room where they may tack on a per-call service charge.

🐦 Always take advantage of the complimentary breakfasts offered by your hotel; even if it's only continental, it will at least pacify you until lunch.

🐦 Consider picking up an *Entertainment* book, either for your home town—it'll still list hotels nationwide—or for your honeymoon destination so you can use restaurant and other coupons, too.

🐦 Avoid the high cost of a taxi; take advantage of your hotel's shuttle service or public transportation instead.

🐦 Tell everyone you're on your honeymoon—you'll be surprised how many freebies this news will bring!

I have one more tip for you—it doesn't have anything to do with saving money, but with coping and saving your sanity as you plan your wedding and honeymoon. If you're like most grooms, you will begin to feel a little helpless as you watch your dear bride and her mother rising to the top of the stress meter as they become immersed in the hundreds of decisions and arrangements that need to be made. And, unfortunately, the tighter the wedding budget, the more they will be trying to do themselves, which adds to the anxiety. So, what can you do to help? Here are a few suggestions:

🐦 Offer to help delegate some of their responsibilities.

🐦 Offer to help with the calling; for example, you can telephone caterers, dance bands, photographers, etc. asking for price quotes or brochures.

🐦 Help assemble the guest list, especially from your side of the family.

🐦 Help your fiancée write thank-you notes. (Yes, this is one of your duties, especially when the gift comes from one of your relatives!)

🐦 Take your bride by the hand and "run away from home" as often as you can; she needs a break from the planning once in a while or she will burn out.

Keep your sense of humor and encourage your bride to "lighten up"; after all, your object is to become man and wife, and as long as that is accomplished, a couple of little snafus won't really matter anyway.

By now, your notebook is full of jots and scribbles and you are more than ready for the "bottom line." This we will finally cover in the next chapter where you will have the opportunity to determine your own personal wedding budget. If this book has encouraged you in the way I intended, you must suspect what I already know—the next chapter will help you devise the perfect plan for you!

I wish you the best as you plan your wedding and honeymoon!

12

Bottom-Line Time

(Budget for All Price Ranges)

This is the chapter you have been waiting for! Finally, you will be able to set up your own wedding budget. I will help you determine how much money you will have and how you should spend it.

I have taken all the cost-cutting plans for each category and arranged them for your consideration. You will need to choose one "plan" from each of the thirteen categories.

Bride's Dress

Something Borrowed	$ 50
Rent It	100
Prom It	100
Bridesmaid's Gown in White	120
Distress-Sale Dress	100
Free Seamstress	195
Hire a Seamstress	321
Buy from a Resale Shop	50-75% off retail
Buy Discount	50 +
The Bridal Suit	150

Bride's Headpiece and Veil

Something Borrowed	$ 0
Rent It	20
Distress Sale	20
Free Seamstress	15
Hire a Seamstress	50
Buy Discount	75

Bride's Slip

Something Borrowed	$ 0
Rent It	10-15
Free Seamstress	10
Hire a Seamstress	30
Buy Discount	40

Bride's Shoes

Something Borrowed	$ 0
Buy Discount	20
Buy Skimmers	20

Flowers

Free Florist	$ 112
Fool Them with Silks	224
Supermarket Wedding Package	250
Fool Them with the Real Thing	300
The Combination Plan	475
Share the Joy	485

Reception Food

The Family Plan	$ 105
Cake and Beverage Only	363
The Pro-Am Combo	594
Amateur Hor d'Oeuvres	777
Amateur Breakfast Buffet	756
Amateur Luncheon Buffet	939
Amateur Dinner Buffet	1,065
Hire the Parish Crew	2,400

Wedding Cake

Dummy Cake + Donated Sheet Cakes	$ 65
Dummy Cake + Bake-Your-Own Sheet Cakes	110
Buy a Supermarket Cake	150
Buy from a Private Party	175
Smaller Wedding Cake + Side Cakes	190

Ceremony Music

Free Recital	$ 0
Pro-Am Combo	40
Canned and Fresh	40
All Local Talent	120

Reception Music

Free Recital	$ 0
Piped-in Music	0
Amateur DJ	0
Party Tapes	0
Two-for-One-Sale	75
All Local Talent	200

Decorations $ 125

Photography

Amateur Photographer	$ 120
Amateur with Rented Camera	170
Artistry Only	350
Find a Reasonable Photographer	600

Videography

Amateur Videographer	$ 10
Amateur with Rented Camera	50
Two Amateurs with Rented Cameras	100
Find a Reasonable Videographer	200

Potpourri $ 677

This is *your* menu. The choices you make from this menu are *your* choices—not your friend's or your aunt's or sister's. Only you know what is important to you. Only you know your own emotions. When you arrive at your final budget, it will be uniquely yours. You will need to weigh each category and select a plan that suits you. In some cases you may even decide to pay full retail price and save in other ways. In any case, don't let anyone rob you of the privilege of making your own decisions.

Beware of the well-meaning people in your life who will try to influence you, some with blatant advice, others with a more subtle approach. Your Aunt Minnie may chastise you in her own ''sweet'' way with, ''You certainly aren't going to wear a homemade dress, are you?'' Perhaps she was a ''Depression child,'' always wore hand-me-downs, and is enjoying your planning for vicarious reasons. She wants you to have a new dress off the rack, regardless of cost. However, unless she plans to pay for it, don't let her remarks influence you. If ever there was a time in your life when you need to keep your head and stand on your own integrity, it is now. If you decide to have your wedding dress sewn for you, it is your decision.

One bride I spoke with recently said she couldn't care less about having a wedding dress around the house for the next forty years, so she decided to rent one. Her only goal was to look fabulous on her wedding day. She let the photographer capture the memories of her dress and she spent the money saved on a great reception party!

Another bride, who happens to be Assyrian, had very sentimental feelings about her dress. It seems that it is traditional in her family to ''embalm'' the dress and then drag it out for future generations to fondle and goggle. She did want to save money, however, so she chose to have her dress sewn.

You will need to make up your own mind about your dress, as well as all your other purchases. You may feel strongly that the sanctuary should be loaded to capacity with professionally arranged flower baskets even if it does leave meager funds for the reception. Or you may be determined to put on an award-winning feast for your guests while filling the church with free lilacs from grandma's backyard.

As you can see, you must make choices. What feels right to you? What means the most? You may find it helpful to take a piece of paper, draw a line down the middle, and make two lists. On the left side of the paper, write down the things that mean the most to you. On the right side of the paper, write down the things that are less important.

Sit back and look at your lists. They will help you create your very own personalized wedding budget from the plans offered in the menu above. Just remember that to spend ''more'' doesn't necessarily mean ''better.''

To give you an idea of how this will work, I have randomly selected various plans from the menu that resulted in the sample budgets that follow. Remember, these budgets are only *examples*. Your budget may not resemble any of them, but the samples will demonstrate how easy it is to construct budgets within various price ranges.

THE ''I FEEL LIKE I JUST WON THE LOTTERY!'' BUDGET $1,374

Bride's Dress, ''Rent It''	$ 100
Bride's Veil, ''Rent It''	20
Bride's Slip, ''Rent It''	20
Bride's Shoes, ''Buy Discount''	20
Flowers, ''Free Florist''	112
Reception Food, ''The Family Plan''	105
Wedding Cake, ''Dummy Cake + Donated''	65
Ceremony Music, ''Free Recital''	0

Reception Music, "Free Recital"	0
Decorations	125
Photography, "Amateur Photographer"	120
Videography, "Amateur Videographer"	10
Potpourri	677
Total	$1,374

THE "NO ONE WILL EVER BELIEVE IT" BUDGET $1,875

Bride's Dress, "Bridesmaid's Dress in White"	$ 120
Bride's Veil, "Free Seamstress"	15
Bride's Slip, "Free Seamstress"	10
Bride's Shoes, "Buy Skimmers"	20
Flowers, "Fool Them with Silks"	224
Reception Food, "Cake and Beverage Only"	364
Wedding Cake, "Dummy Cake + Bake Your Own"	110
Ceremony Music, "Pro-Am Combo"	40
Reception Music, "Amateur DJ"	0
Decorations	125
Photography, "Amateur Photographer"	120
Videographer, "Amateur with Rented Camera"	50
Potpourri	677
Total	$1,875

THE "BIG SIGH OF RELIEF" BUDGET $2,100

Bride's Dress, "The Distress Sale Dress"	$ 100
Bride's Veil, "The Distress Sale Veil"	20
Bride's Slip, "Free Seamstress"	10
Bride's Shoes, "Buy Skimmers"	20
Flowers, "Fool Them with the Real Thing"	300
Reception Food, "Cake and Beverage Only"	363
Wedding Cake, "Buy from a Private Party"	175

Ceremony Music, "Pro-Am Combo"	40
Reception Music, "Amateur DJ"	0
Decorations	125
Photography, "Amateur with Rented Camera"	170
Videography, "Two Amateurs with Rented Cameras"	100
Potpourri	677
Total	$2,100

THE "CAN'T STOP GRINNING" BUDGET $2,832

Bride's Dress, "Hire a Seamstress"	$ 321
Bride's Veil, "Hire a Seamstress"	50
Bride's Slip, "Hire a Seamstress"	30
Bride's Shoes, "Buy Skimmers"	20
Flowers, "Fool Them with the Real Thing"	300
Reception Food, "The Pro-Am Combo"	594
Wedding Cake, "Buy a Supermarket Cake"	150
Ceremony Music, "Pro-Am Combo"	40
Reception Music, "Two-for-One Sale"	75
Decorations	125
Photography, "Artistry Only"	350
Videography, "Two Amateurs with Rented Cameras"	100
Potpourri	677
Total	$2,832

THE "GET TO KEEP THE CAR AFTER ALL" BUDGET $3,445

Bride's Dress, "Hire a Seamstress"	$ 321
Bride's Veil, "Buy Discount"	75
Bride's Slip, "Hire a Seamstress"	30
Bride's Shoes, "Buy Skimmers"	20
Flowers, "Share the Joy"	485

Reception Food, "Amateur Hors d'Oeuvres"	777
Wedding Cake, "Smaller Cake + Side Cakes"	190
Ceremony Music, "All Local Talent"	120
Reception Music, "Two-for-One-Sale"	75
Decorations	125
Photography, "Artistry Only"	350
Videography, "Find a Reasonable Videographer"	200
Potpourri	677
Total	$3,445

THE "MONEY LEFT OVER FOR A HONEYMOON" BUDGET $5,528

Bride's Dress, "Hire a Seamstress"	$ 321
Bride's Veil (Buy retail)	150
Bride's Slip, "Buy Discount"	40
Bride's Shoes, "Buy Skimmers"	20
Flowers, "Share the Joy"	485
Reception Food, "Hire the Parish Crew"	2,400
Wedding Cake, "Smaller Cake + Side Cakes"	190
Ceremony Music, "All Local Talent"	120
Reception Music, "All Local Talent"	200
Decorations	125
Photography, "Find a Reasonable Photographer"	600
Videography, "Find a Reasonable Videographer"	200
Potpourri	677
Total	$5,528

THE "RICH AND FAMOUS EVEN LOVE IT" BUDGET $7,242

Bride's Dress (Buy retail)	$1,100
Bride's Veil (Buy retail)	150
Bride's Slip (Buy retail)	60

Bride's Shoes (Buy retail)	60
Flowers (Pay full retail price)	1,000
Reception Food, "Hire the Parish Crew"	2,400
Wedding Cake (Buy retail)	550
Ceremony Music, "All Local Talent"	120
Reception Music, "All Local Talent"	200
Decorations	125
Photography, "Find a Reasonable Photographer"	600
Videography, "Find a Reasonable Videographer"	200
Potpourri	677
Total	$7,242

As you look at these budgets and realize how much money you can save on your wedding, I'm sure you're wondering if it is really, honest-to-goodness possible to pull this off. I can tell you without reservation that it is. After hearing from so many brides in response to this book, and after serving as a consultant and seminar leader to hundreds of couples as well, I can tell you for a fact that thousands upon thousands of dollars have been saved, without jeopardizing the quaility of the weddings.

Because this is exactly what I want for you—a high quality wedding on an affordable budget—I thought you might appreciate seeing excerpts of a few of the thousands of letters I have received from brides who have used the ideas in this book.

Here are four true stories of "big weddings on small budgets":

NASHVILLE, NORTH CAROLINA Total Cost: $3,000

The bride received a copy of this book from her fiancé at the same time she received her engagement ring. She wrote that the book "allowed us to have 'classy' wedding at an inexpensive price."

Here are some of the ways that did it:

- ❦ Bridesmaids' bouquets homemade of white silk flowers, embellished with ivy, string pearls by-the-yard and a hot glue gun.

- ❦ Homemade ring bearer's pillow.

- ❦ Boutonnieres made by the bride and her mother several months before the wedding from packaged silk flowers, imitation rose leaves and a little baby's breath.

- Candles purchased from a wholesale candle outlet that were "cheaper by the dozen."

- Ceremony site decorated with fresh greenery stripped from cedar trees in the North Carolina mountains (several garbage bags full) and "tied together" with floral wire.

- Bride's veil made by her mother at a cost of $13, a copy of one they had seen in a salon for about $150.

- Bride's gown purchased at 50 percent off retail at an outlet store in Reading, Ohio.

- Used a professional florist only for the center table arrangement at the reception, the bride's going-away corsage and one large arrangement for the front of the church. Total cost: $85.

- Bride's father made the kneeling bench, which was donated to the church after the wedding.

- They used the existing Christmas "plug-in" candles, plus added greenery and a white bow to all eight windows. Bows were also added to the first three pews.

- The bride and her fiancé decorated the reception site the day before the wedding (pinned netting, ribbons, bows and great swags of tulle across the fronts of all the tables).

- The reception food was made by the bride, the bride's mother and a friend of the family. Another friend served as a supervisor to help keep the trays filled during the reception.

- Professional cake; paid $180. It had two sections joined by a stairway. One section had four layers and the other three, plus they added one large Styrofoam layer to give the cake a higher, more dramatic look.

- Used a professional photographer.

The bride wrote, "David and I cannot thank you enough for your input in our wedding. The entire sha-bang was only $3,000 . . . my sister spent more than that on her reception alone." Because they saved so much on their wedding, they were able to splurge on their honeymoon—a Western Caribbean cruise.

By the way, their only wedding glitch involved the photographer's equipment and the bridesmaids' street clothes which had been locked into a dressing room, for which there was *no* key! The bride wrote, "The custodian had no key; the preacher had no key; the church secretary had no key. My brother-in-law opened the door with a credit card, and I thought that was only in the movies!"

BALTIMORE, MARYLAND   Total Cost: $3,731

Believe it or not, this couple's wedding and honeymoon *combined* totaled $3,731, and here are some of the clever things they did to pull this off:

- Purchased the bride's gown off a sale rack at a bridal salon for $282. (She saw the identical gown at another shop for $750 retail.)

- Alterations done for free by groom's mother who also made the bride's petticoat for $17 and a "gorgeous" headpiece and veil for $25.

- Bride wore her own white flat shoes and jewelry.

- Purchased bridesmaids' dresses from a JCPenney outlet store for under $50 each. (She wrote that some were as low as $30.)

- Wedding cake baked by a woman who bakes cakes at her home; charged $.84 per slice. (The usual retail bakery in her area charges from $1 to $3 per slice.)

- They found a restaurant with a "gorgeous, waterfront location," where brunch was served at $8 per person, which included free use of a room for the ceremony itself, plus use of an outside deck. The bride wrote, "The location had a spectacular view with the early morning sunlight dancing on the water and the boats all around the marina. . . . I'm sure our guests must have thought we spent a fortune." By the way, the $8 figure is $4 off the restaurant's regular brunch menu price because the bride "negotiated away" some of the fancier items, such as the Eggs Benedict topped with crab, which left them scrambled eggs, bacon, sausage, home fries, muffins, bagels with cream cheese, pancakes, French toast, a beautiful fruit display, coffee, tea and orange juice. (The bride said that in the Baltimore/Washington, DC metro area you would usually pay as little as $10 to as much as $130 per person, with $40 being the average.)

- The bride purchased blank invitations (in packages of 50 for $6) at a stationery outlet, and a friend had them printed as a gift.

- All the flowers were free—a gift from a member of their family who happens to be a professional florist. (At first, he was going to sell them the flowers at his wholesale cost of $100, but just days before the wedding he told the bride that the flowers would be his gift to them.)

- Photography and videography—all done by friends and family members who were amateurs.

- Played taped music for the reception.

The bride wrote, "I never felt more special or beautiful than I did on my wedding day, and when my husband saw me coming down the aisle, he got misty and looked at me like he never had before. When it comes right down to it, *that* is what weddings are all about—not how much you spend! We saved so much money that we could afford a week-long honeymoon on the sunny beaches of Florida. By going off-season we saved tons of money there as well. We spent a Grand Total of $3,731 on the entire wedding and honeymoon *combined*! I'm sure everyone thought we spent thousands more. With a little creativity and ingenuity, other couples will be able to do it, too. I know it sounds hopelessly cliché, but if we can do it, just about anyone can!"

CLEWISTON, FLORIDA   Total Cost: $2,723

David and Jennifer Cook met in Vacation Bible School when they were children; they were friends and eventually fell in love and decided to get married, which they did for a total cost of only $2,723. I first heard about this wedding when the bride's mother wrote me, thanking me for the book, and enclosing a beautiful photograph of Jennifer and several pages telling how they managed such an exquisite wedding for so little money. Here are the highlights of her letter:

Bride's gown (purchased new)	$463
Bride's veil (wore her mother's)	0
Bride's slip	25
Bride's shoes (purchased at the "Dollar Store")	5
Shoe decorations	10
Mother-of-the-bride's dress (borrowed)	0
Maide of Honor's beaded dress (borrowed)	0
Bride's floral bouquet (Created by her aunt from supermarket flowers and ivy, pink day lilies and ivory roses from her yard.)	50
Church decorations	170

Reception food (prepared by family and friends)	550
Wedding cake (baked by a friend), decorations only	20
Band for the reception	400
Misc. decorations (ribbon, lace, etc.)	125
Tablecloth and aisle runner	30
Nursery care	30
Photography (by an amateur friend)	0
Videography (given as a wedding gift)	0
Bride's photograph only (professional)	150
225 invitations (could have saved money if would have ordered enough the first time; the re-order was expensive)	280
Champagne (1 case)	38
Thank-you notes	24
Napkins (not printed)	10
Postage	60
Church sound man (a family member)	0
Favors (Hershey's Kisses)	25
2 garters	12
Guest book	6
Ring bearer pillow	7
Makeup for bride, maid-of-honor and mother-of-bride (Mary Kay rep did the makeup for free)	0
Organist	40
CDs for soloist	45
Gifts (bride's mother makes porcelain dolls and gave some as gifts)	80
Headpieces for maid of honor and flower girl (made by bride's aunt from supermarket flowers and ivy from her yard)	3
Paper products (from Sam's Club)	65

By the way, you should see the bride's bouquet made by her aunt. It is so expensive looking!

Although this couple lives in Seattle, they had to plan a long-distance wedding because both their families live in Montana. The bride wrote, "This was a challenge at times, but having a wedding there (in Butte) instead of Seattle saved us quite a lot."

There were 250 guests at the wedding, and this is exactly what the couple spent:

Bride's gown, sewn by a Seattle seamstress	$400
Bride's makeup and hair, done by a friend	0
Rented hoop petticoat	8
Veil, made by the bride	15
Shoes & hosiery, discount	30
Rented bridesmaids' dresses (split the cost)	50
Bridesmaids' & groomsmen's gifts (6 @ $20)	120
Reception hall rental	250
Photographer (a retired man with experience)	265
Cake (baked by a private party)	150
Video (by bride's brother)	0
Caterer (a family friend who runs a catering business out of her home, @ $2.50 per person)	675
DJ (for reception)	225
Minister's fee (bride's father)	0
Organist & soloist (friends of the family who performed for free, but bride bought gifts)	30
Trumpeters (2)	120
Flowers (the bride made them up in silks ahead of time—shopped discount)	200
Decorations, balloons & misc.	100
Groom's tuxedo, plus split cost of groomsmens'	150
Potpourri	600

The bride wrote that the only problem on her wedding day was that the hoop skirt didn't work well under her wedding gown (she had neglected to try it on ahead of time!) which resulted in a full hour's worth of emergency "fixins" right before the service began. Other than that, everything went off without a hitch and, if the photographs are any indication, the wedding had an elegant, expensive look and the bride was beautiful, cranky hoop skirt, or not!

Finally, I thought you might enjoy seeing a breakdown of the costs for our daughter's wedding, which totaled $3,530:

Bridal Attire

Wedding dress	$ 400
Veil	120
Slip	50
Shoes	24

Florist	289
Reception Food	990
Wedding Cake	185

Music

One vocalist	25
Four musicians @ $40	160

Decorations	110
Nursery Care	45
Photography	500
Videography (Gift)	0

Potpourri

Ice sculpture	50
225 Invitations	85
300 Napkins	35
Thank-you notes	24
Postage	60
Church custodian	50
Church sound man	25
Church coordinator	35
Favors	20
Slide developing (for reception slide show)	15
Dry-cleaning bills (last-minute pressing)	24
Last-minute alterations	25
Throw-away garter	5
Supermarket flowers (for cake and buffet table)	18
Bride's blood test and exam	40
Guest book	6
Ring bearer's pillow	7

Special calligraphy pen	10
Mints	10
Hair appointments	36
Sheet music/organist	6
Bridesmaids' headpieces	6
Paper plates/forks for cake	28
Baskets for distributing favors	12
Total	**$3,530**

As you will recall from the Introduction, we faced these expenses at a time when we were not prepared; we definitely did not have a "wedding fund" as we should have. However, because our daughter paid for all her own wedding clothes, and the groom's parents generously helped toward the reception food, we were able to squeeze the money out of our budget over a four-month period. This meant that our law-student son needed to borrow a little more than he had planned on that year's student loan, but he was more than happy to do this. So it all worked out, paying cash as we went.

How are you going to handle your wedding expenses? You can juggle things around as we did, or I have some other suggestions:

Do you have any savings bonds you can sell?

Do you have any other available savings you can use?

Do you have an extra vehicle you can sell?

How about the small lot you inherited from Uncle Octavio several years ago? Could it be sold quickly?

Do you have an insurance policy with cash value?

How about the stamp, baseball card or coin collection?

Why not have a huge family garage sale? Ask the relatives if they would donate their castaways to the cause. People will buy anything!

What about borrowing money? This is a very serious question because you don't want the emotion of the moment to leave you with a debt that will become a serious burden to your family after the wedding. Be very careful!

Remember the first section of your notebook called "The Budget"? This is where you will need to enter the exact budget plan you have selected, as well as the source of monies you will have available. You should also enter the dollar amount for each category at the top of the other sections in your notebook. Keep these figures close to your heart as you are out and about making your purchases; then enter your actual purchases in your notebook daily so that you will know where you stand all the time.

One word of caution to the mother of the bride: Don't get caught in the trap of trying to give your daughter a wedding that is what you really wanted when you were married, but didn't have. It is so easy to get caught up in vicarious planning—living out the romance and excitement through your daughter. Believe me, if you stay on the budget you select, she will be just as happy a year from now than if you had lost your head and gone out of control, and you won't have all those bills to pay!

This is a time for mature restraint, but it can still be one of the most rewarding and creative things you have ever done! You'll see!

13

I Think I Can,
I Think I Can . . .

(Putting It All Together)

Have you ever watched a group of women as they make a personalized quilt? They lovingly and painstakingly create individual squares that are finally sewn together. In the beginning stages the quilt doesn't look like much, but the individual squares form a true work of art as they are fitted together. During this process a peculiar thing happens—the underside becomes quite a mess. There are wads of strings and knots and, seemingly, no pattern at all. And yet, if it weren't for these ugly, messy pieces of thread and yarn, there could never be the pretty design on top.

Your wedding plans will seem at times like a quilt. One of the squares will have a flower on it; you will work patiently on this square until it finally looks good enough to add to the rest of your handiwork. Your food square will be full of tiny details and it will also take patience, but when it is complete, it, too, will be ready to join your other lovely squares.

As you are working along, the underside of your quilt will become a mass of strings and knots. Your floral square might have a dangling strand of ribbon, exchanged three times before its color seemed exactly right; your food square may have a big knot caused by your frustration and indecision. From time to time, your life in general may even seem like strings and knots, for occasionally your mind will feel cluttered and often your den will be, too. You will have price lists sitting on top of catalogs, and pictures of wedding cakes intermingled with the fabric you purchased to make the covered umbrellas. But when things seem confusing, just say to yourself, "I'm only looking at the back of the quilt!" However, the time will come, and sooner than you think, when you will be able to stand back and see the finished product. What a thrill that will be for you!

Meanwhile, diligently use your notebook. Accept and enjoy your role as wedding coordinator. Consider it a great privilege and opportunity to be able to use your abilities in this way. And remember that all your expertise won't go to waste, for perhaps you will have another wedding to plan some day, or you may even have a dear friend who needs your help. The knowledge and experience you will gain through this planning can be wonderfully useful in the future.

Just consider yourself a master quilter as you make those phone calls, talk to those florists and tie up the pew bows. All the pieces will come together in the end and it will be worth all the work.

I have been through this entire creative process, so I have empathy for you. I have stood at the beginning, where you are standing now, with all of your questions and frustrations. But, I made it through to the end where I was able to stand back and admire my beautiful quilt!

Your quilt will be a beauty and it will probably win a prize. I can see it now:

FIRST PRIZE
for
Patience
and
Creativity

Remember the positive attitude we talked about in the first chapter? Now is the time to kick it into gear! Put that smile on your face and remember that I'm cheering for you!

You can do it!

Index

bridesmaids' dress, 45-46
bridesmaids' slip, 49
camera, 110
ceremony and reception site, 121-124
decoration, 105
floral arrangement, 66
mother's dress, 43
private, for honeymoon, 145
tuxedo, 51-52
video camera, 118
wedding dress, 31
Resale shop, buying wedding dress at, 35
Ring. *See* Engagement ring, Wedding bands
Ring bearer, 52-53
pillow for, 131
Rose garden theme, 96
RV, honeymoon in, 143-144

S
Schedule. *See* Calendar
Seamstress
for bride's headpiece, 39
for bride's slip, 40
for bridesmaids' slips, 49
for bridesmaids' dresses, 47
for flower girl's dress, 51
for mother's dress, 44
for wedding dress, 35
Seed packets, decorated, 128
Sewing
bride's headpiece, 37
bride's slip, 39-40
bridesmaids' dresses, 46-47
bridesmaids' headpieces, 48
bridesmaids' slips, 49
flower girl's dress, 50
mother's dress, 43-44
wedding dress, 33-34
Shoes
bride's, 40-41
bridesmaids', 49
choosing plan for, 150
Silk flowers, 60-63
Skimmers, 41, 49

Slip
bride's, 39-40
bridesmaid's, 48-49
choosing plan for, 150
Snowball wedding, 100
Soaps, netted, 127
Suit
bridal, 36
for groomsmen, 52
See also Going-away outfit
Supermarket
cake from, 83
floral package, 64-65
Surprise ceremony, 7
Synagogue. *See* Church or synagogue

T
Table
buffet, 79-81
skirts for, 131
Thank-you notes, 124
written by groom, 147
Themes, 19, 94-106
importance of, 94-96
Timetable. *See* Calendar
Tips
for amateur photographer, 112-114
for amateur videographer, 119-120
for cutting honeymoon costs, 146-147
Traditional themes
decorations for, 103
for reception, 96-97
Travel wedding, 6-7
Trends
in candid photography, 116-117
in weddings, 5-7
See also Nontraditional themes
Tussie-mussie bouquet, 68
Tuxedos, 51-52

U
Ushers. *See* Groomsmen

To the Reader

I will be updating this book constantly and could use your help. Please write me and let me know how this book worked for you. Send me your own unique cost-cutting ideas and any price variations you found in your region. Also, I have a big bulletin board in my office for my readers' wedding photos. Do you have an extra for me?
Thanks so much,

Diane Warner
% Betterway Books
1507 Dana Avenue
Cincinnati, Ohio 45207